The MEANING *Of* LIFE

SAMPSON OFORI YIADOM

Printed by NABERM PUBLICATIONS

ISBN: 9-781-733-189-033

NABERM
PUBLICATIONS

NABERM Publications
6564 Loisdale Ct. ste 600, Springfield VA 22150
Or
P.O. Box 513, Owings Mills MD 21117
703-468-7058
Nabermpublications@gmail.com
Nabermpublications.com

Cover and Layout by:
Hetura Company Limited

DEDICATION

I dedicate this book to my father Rev. Emmanuel Kwaku Ofosu (Rtd), of the Church of Pentecost, whose godly life, faithful ministry and commitment to God led to my salvation and training in the fear of God. Also, to my dear wife, Millicent whose incessant support and encouragement helped to prepare me for the writing of this book, and to my children – Emmanuel, Noel, Sebastien and Jeffrey – whose sacrifices and understanding have been a blessing to my ministry.

TABLE OF CONTENTS

FOREWORD

The primordial questions about life continue to engage the discussions of great philosophers over the centuries. From where did we come here; why are we here on earth; where do we go from here; why do we die; is there life after death, if so, what kind of life is it; is there God; if God is love why is there so much suffering, injustice and evil in the world; what is therefore the meaning and purpose of life?

Greek philosophers who lived 400 to 300 years BCE, like Socrates, Aristotle, Plato, Epicurus, as well as others like Chinese philosopher, Confucius, propounded many wise sayings in a bid to defining the nature and meaning of life. The celebrated English literary genius, William Shakespeare (1564--1616), is listed among the best who proffered very many ideas about the nature and meaning of life. In his book, Macbeth, Shakespeare wrote:

> *"...Life is a brief candle...*
> *A walking shadow...*
> *It is a tale told by an idiot,*
> *Full of sound and fury,*
> *Signifying nothing."*

Then in another book, As You Like It, Shakespeare penned the famous saying, often paraphrased as:

"The world is a stage
And all of us are actors
We have our entrance and our exit
And are heard no more."

But long before the birth of Jesus Christ a young man became king in Israel in 970 BCE. His name was King Solomon. His God-given wisdom made him the wisest man who ever lived. He spoke 3,000 proverbs and wrote 1,005 songs (1 Kings 4:29-34), including the Biblical books of Proverbs, Ecclesiastes, and Songs of Solomon. He wrote about very many things...from the stately cedars of Lebanon to the smallest shrubs growing on walls, about animals, insects, marine creatures, to flying creatures. He wrote about life, its nature, purpose and vicissitudes. He was the quintessence of knowledge and of wisdom. Consequently, any study of the subject of Life ...its meaning and purpose... without recourse to Solomon, would be inconclusive and parochial.

In this small but relevant book, THE MEANING OF LIFE, Apostle Sampson Ofori Yiadom, the author, draws heavily on the book of Ecclesiastes to distil the meaning and purpose of life. From his personal and pastoral perspectives this young, astute, and seasoned apostle with very keen spiritual binoculars and sensors, unravels the meanings of Solomon's apparent, sombre description of life and its circumstances as "Vanity of vanities" as "Meaningless" and a "Chasing after the wind." He asserts that if life and its purposes are defined in the Solomonic pleasure-hunt for the gratification of fleshly desires, the result of such a life would suit Solomon's description of ...Vanity... Meaningless...a Chasing after the wind. Such a lifestyle has its consequences...it engenders a plethora of human woes and ultimately terminates in death.

On the other hand, the author posits that since God is the Originator and Source of life, every proper definition of life must begin with His perspectives. God made us for Himself, for His pleasure, for fellowship with Himself. He made us in His own image, gave us dominion, and made us stewards of His entire Creation. When man blew up this glorious estate, God sent His Son Jesus Christ to restore this Life to us, who gave not just life but ABUNDANT LIFE!! Hence life's meaninglessness and vanity lamented by Solomon finds its ultimate solution in Christ Jesus. Apostle Yiadom concludes on the hearty note that life in Christ can be meaningful, purposeful, rewarding. Oh, what a book !! Small but laden with deep spiritual insight and revelation. I heartily recommend to all.

APOSTLE DR MICHAEL NTUMY

(Order of the Volta, Companion: A Ghanaian Presidential Award)
* Chairman, The Church of Pentecost (1998-2008)
* President, Ghana Pentecostal and Charismatic Council (1998-2008)
* President, Bible Society of Ghana (2006-2008)
* Chancellor, Pentecost University College (2003-2008)

PREFACE

True fulfilment and life's meaning come from knowing God and walking with him faithfully. In the book- *The Meaning of Life*- this argument is made and supported by the Word of God; as well as, external sources, including scholarly sources. People hold the perception that life is war, a struggle, and how you make it among others. This author pursues lessons presented by King Solomon in the book of Ecclesiastes in the Bible and addresses how the Word of God can be utilized to settle the confusion surrounding the meaninglessness of life. The author invites readers to reflect on aspects of this conversation.

The key objective of the book is to draw extensively on King Solomon's' experiences to explore the meaning of life by observing the overarching thesis that life with God is not vanity or meaningless. The promise of the book is to examine the asymmetric association between God and man by drawing conclusions and analogies from man's earthly existence. For this reason, the author poses practical and useful questions as part of a purposeful engagement with readers.

The book is a *step-by-step* guide to the meaning of life with an introduction and conclusion pages; as well as, a systematic approach chosen for the 11 themes, as follows: the meaning of life, the concept of life, choices become life, Life without God, the profitability of life, the fear of God is key, figuring it out, there is nothing new under the sun, Christ gives meaning to life, the seasons of life, and living abundant life. The Chapter disposition is provided below.

Chapter 1 of the book is devoted to a discussion on the definition of life from several angles; including religious, philosophical, and cultural backgrounds. The author makes two profound arguments: (i) God is not in the knowledge of philosophy because such thoughts are not checked with the Word of God; (ii) the extrapolation of meaning of life from the Bible is not philosophy. In Chapter 2, the author rejects the theory of evolution because life is not accidental and establishes that Jesus gave life both in form and shape and supported the argument with John 1:1-5 to establish God's definition of life. Additionally, the author determines that human life is of immeasurable value created in God's image and conferred with dominion and stewardship. In Chapter 3, the author compares the life of Solomon to that of Joseph in the Bible to make a case for making right choices towards fulfilled destinies. While Joseph made right choices covering his faithfulness in the teeth of opposition and adversity; Solomon made wrong choices involving his marriages to foreign women and later regretted. Actions have consequences.

Chapter 4 is largely taken up in response to what happens when we repudiate God's authority over our lives. Here, the emphasis is that God is not responsible for suffering, negativity of life, and chaos; but the cause of suffering is traceable to the fall of man (Adam and Eve). The question is: Why blame God for sufferings? Solomon's realistic outlook of life and the use of the fear of God as a weapon for mastering the affairs of life are explored in chapter 5 of the book. In Chapter 6, the importance of the fear of God as a key variable for properly functioning in wisdom is recounted, using David's grateful heart through his fear of God, faith in God, and gratefulness to God; as well as, Abraham's trust in the sovereignty of God.

There is the need to figure out man's meaningful life by concentrating on identity, heritage, purpose, destiny, and utilization of abilities, gifts, and potentials. Questions bordering on these variables are discussed in Chapter 7. Finding meaning in life is to figure out what one is destined to do and to allow the Lord to bring that meaning into fruition. The noticeable theme is explored in Chapter 8, where the author argues that there are discoveries instead of inventions by concurring with Solomon that "there is nothing new under the sun" because the inventions of light bulbs, irrigation, airplane, submarines, ocean liners, auto doors and many more have their roots in the Bible. However, it is rather the entertainers and entrepreneurs who have attempted to satisfy the cravings of man. Jesus can redeem man from the vanity that Solomon talked about in the book of Ecclesiastes.

Chapter 9-*Christ gives meaning to life*. Solomon adopts a *pastoral* tone in the book of Ecclesiastes to shed lights on this theme bordering on the salvation of man. *First*, the Word gave life to the world (John 1:4), and that people need to gravitate towards God in prayer, reading of Scriptures, handling of emotions, and conversations; because life without God is valueless. The Biblical story of Lazarus and the rich man is applied to establish that it is appointed unto man to die but riches cannot be relied upon for salvation. *Second*, emptiness is a separation between oneself and the creator and there is hope for the Christian even after death. The summary of the book of Ecclesiastes is the very last Chapter. *Three*, Christ's redemptive act is a divine key to unlock the doors to a meaningful life; as a result, while the past age looked forward to Christ's redemptive works, the present age looks back on Christ's completed works. *Four*, sins are forgiven because "*it is finished*" in the past, the present, and the future. Serving God and pursuing the will of God for life is of utmost priority. *Lastly*, a renewed call is to make a new start because true fulfilment and life's meaning come from knowing God and walking faithfully with Him.

This book is to provide guidance on daily Christian living because in Chapter 10, the author explores the seasons of life, with emphasis on the rotation and revolution of the earth that provides: day and night; as well as the four seasons. The development that has taken place is to allow for man to co-operate with God's timing to have meaningful life, and to learn the secrets of a successful life from God's principles. Chapter 11 returns to living abundant life. The following major points have been discussed: *One,* many Christians are ridiculed by the world as being dull, out of touch, humourless, and boring; and for this reason, some churches have responded to this by integrating modernity into the mode of worship. *Two*, exercising self-control does not make life boring, unrewarding, or under-privileged; because abundant life means different things to different people. Abundant life is as Christ lived it- Knowing God.

In the closing chapter, a way is suggested for a solid relationship with the Creator to be built as a key to abundant life because the real meaning of life is implicit in Matthew 6:19-34, with emphasis on -*do not store up* and *do not worry*-There is the need to have the rule of God in man's heart. Even though, bad choices may have been made in the past, if man becomes born of God and accepts Jesus Christ into his or her life, God's likeness will be restored. A call is made for man to reflect on Christ in whatever is done on earth.

The book is intended to fill a gap in the literature on the meaning of life. The book remains consistent with the writer's desire to provide a *construct* on the meaning of life. Several historical accounts have been provided in some chapters as important component of the book. This is a helpful book, clearly argued with interesting themes covering a solid collection aimed at Christians in their appreciation of the meaning of life. A nicely presented book, with discernible themes based on accuracy of scriptural application and interpretation. Where translation from Greek is done, the challenge of the conversation is not implicit in the Greek but rather in its interpretation.

Every academic library, scholar, and people concerned about the meaning of life should own this book. References and direct quotes from the Bible have been provided to assist the readers to appreciate further reading. A very critical area of theology has been captured in this book in response to the need to fear God in order to have peace and fulfilment on earth.

APOSTLE SAMPSON OFORI-YIADOM
September 29, 2019

ACKNOWLEDGMENT

I render all heartfelt gratitude and appreciation to God all Mighty for giving me the grace to write this book. It is nothing short of His divine fulfilment of his word to me. I could never have accomplished this piece without God who by His Spirit, is working in me to accomplish His will.

During my Missions work in Germany, I had the privilege to work with Apostle Dr. M.K Ntumy (Former Chairman of the Church of Pentecost). In one of our discussions he said to me, "Son you have to write a book, you must begin to write the wealth of Knowledge and wisdom which God has inscribed in you". My heart was heavily burdened because, though I had that inclination, it was not something I seriously considered. The burden his advice placed on me, later inspired me to write this book. For this reason, I deem it fit to thank Apostle Dr. M.K Ntumy for his words of encouragement, and also for writing the foreword of the book.

In addition, I owe tones of gratitude to Apostle Professor Opoku Onyinah (Immediate past Chairman of the church of Pentecost), Aps. Eric Nyamekye (The Chairman of the Church), Aps. Alexander Kumi Larbi (The General Secretary), Aps. Emmanuel Gyesi Addo (The IMD), and all fathers, for the impact you continue to have on my life and ministry.

I am eternally grateful to my mentor Apostle Albert Amoah (Rtd) and wife Mama Agartha, for the invaluable contributions they have made in my life.

A special word of gratitude is due to Elder Dr. Appiah-Sokye of Romeoville district who reviewed the book, and breathed into several chapters of the book. You put heart and soul into making these books a reality; I am forever indebted to you.

I am also thankful to the following: Deaconess Dr. Hannah Anokye of Chicago District for helping with the editing of the book, Ms. Bridget Mawusi Amenyo, for helping with proof reading and typing some of the materials, all Ministers of the Chicago Region and many others for their immense love, encouragement and support, they kept me going and this book would not have been possible without them.

Last but not the least, I express my profoundest gratitude to the love of my life, a woman of prayer and an encourager, Mrs. Millicent Yiadom for her prayer support and encouragement.

INTRODUCTION

The purpose of this book is to share my personal thoughts based on the Word of God and to give hope to a supposedly life of meaninglessness. I was reading the book of Ecclesiastes as part of my usual Bible study sessions and I was baffled by the pessimistic tone right from the beginning.

Solomon, a man specially gifted by God with wisdom wrote this Book late in his life, following an eventful forty-year reign. Many thoughts run through my mind as to why the writer pronounced vanity on almost everything one can have in this life. I reached a moment of confusion while I pondered on such mind-boggling concepts in the book and therefore, felt burdened to explore the various dimensions of the book. Interestingly, I realized that, the writer like many of us in today's world, was trying to find a secure value in this life that can serve as a blueprint for proper living.

Reading the book, it appears to me that, despite all the efforts he made, he found none. In fact, he tried everything one could possibly indulge in, including science, wisdom, wealth, pleasure, entertainment, and sexual gratification; as well as, power, material things, money, great accomplishments, and many more. They proved to be elusive and fleeting transition.

To the Christian, the book of Ecclesiastes may appear to have a grim beginning, announcing, "vanity of vanities", says the

Preacher: "vanity of vanities, all is vanity" What profit has a man from all his labor in which he toils under the sun?" (Ecclesiastes 1:2-3).

Upon reading the first few chapters of Ecclesiastes, one is tempted to ask why Solomon's outlook of life was decidedly negative; despite living in majestic glory, with every facility to make life interesting. He analyses in detail what life's meaning is, as he lived a very unhappy, regretful, and unfulfilled life; *in spite* of the blessings of God upon his life. He was immensely blessed with everything a man requires for a happy and fulfilled life.

A lot of people misunderstand the real essence of life, thereby setting for themselves what I call *misguided goals*. Some also idle about, thinking that after all, in the end, we are going to leave everything we have toiled for behind and go back to the dust, as naked as we came. Sadly, others too, in an attempt to find out the real meaning of life, get entangled in the lusts of the world, thinking that could guarantee them happiness and fulfilment.

The Book of Ecclesiastes to a great extent presents the Christian with a unique perspective on life. It deals with life's difficulties, pains, struggles and every affair of life. King Solomon reflects on life and relates his experiences for us to draw lessons from.

The question of whether life is worth living or meaningful, is a global discourse that many people are trying to find answers to, but end up getting even more frustrated. For this reason, the burden of finding answers to the meaning of life culminated into the writing of this book.

This is because the search for answers to the meaning of life is not hidden in voluminous books and philosophies. I wish to acknowledge that most of the concepts stated in this book are based on the life of Solomon as recounted in the book of Ecclesiastes. So then, what is life all about? What do you think is the meaning of life? Is life worth living?

O'Donnell (2014) postulated: *"the interdependent tasks of biblical exposition and theological reflection are best undertaken in the church, and most especially in the pulpits of the church. This is all the more, true since the study of Scripture properly results in doxology and praxis-that is, in praise to God and practical application in the lives of believers"* (p.ix). *First,* my desire is to settle the confusion that clouded my mind; and *second,* to also seek clarity for any confused mind to demonstrate that life with God is not vanity upon vanity.

Let's discover possible answers in this book.

CHAPTER ONE

WHAT IS LIFE?

●

The common but complex question millions of people wrestle with is related to the meaning of life, or the answer to the question: *What is the meaning of life?* While life pertains to the significance of living or existence in general; many other issues are involved, such as symbolic meaning, ontology (the structure of nature reality study); value, purpose, ethics, good and evil, freewill, conceptions of God, the soul, and the *afterlife*. There is an answer to the question of what life is but until the seemingly-imperfect, good and evil-afflicted human condition is explained, the meaning of life cannot be acknowledged (Griffith, 2011-2016, p.70). In this chapter, the meaning of life will be explored.

Life Defined

Life is (i) the quality that distinguishes a vital and functional being from a dead body; (ii) the sequence of physical and mental experiences that make up the existence of an individual; (iii) spiritual existence transcending physical death and the craving for the release into the life to come; and (iv) the period from birth to death (Merriam-Webster Dictionary, 1828). The dictionary definition of life is varied but few will be emphasized:

1. Life is *the qualities that distinguishes a vital and functional being from a dead body*; (b) a principle or force that is considered to underlie the distinctive quality of animate beings; and (c) one or more aspects of the process of living. (The Merriam Webster's Collegiate Dictionary, Tenth Edition p.672).

2. Life is *the period between birth and death, or the experience or state of being alive* (Retrieved from *https:// dictionary.cambridge.org-accessed on 09/20/2019*)

3. The property or quality that distinguishes living organisms from dead organisms and inanimate matter, manifested in functions such as metabolism, growth, reproduction, and response to stimuli or adaptation to the environment originating from within the organism. (Retrieved from https://www. thefreedictionary.com-accessed on 09/22/2019).

There have been several proposed answers from different cultural backgrounds throughout history, including philosophical, scientific, theological, and metaphysical speculation. A journal by name -*Philosophy Now* in 2019 posed the question for the month: *What is life?* The perspectives of 10 respondents encompassed the following: (1) *reproduction and metabolism*, life is the aspect of existence that processes, acts, reacts, evaluates, and evolves through growth (Anonymous); (2) Tom Baranski of New Jersey explained that life exists at many levels and that life is a process through which energy and materials are transformed, and so is non-life; (3) Nicholas Taylor of Berkshire offered that life is self-organizing chemistry which produces itself and passes on its evolved characteristics, and encoded in DNA; and (4) life is the embodiment of selfishness because it is for itself in two ways-(i) it is for its own survival, and (ii) it is for its own reproduction (Dr. Harry Fuchs of Warwickshire).

(5) Dr. Steve Brewer of Cornwell elaborated that the scientific definition of life is valid in its context but otherwise he finds it impoverished; based on the hypothesis of *Ivan Tyrrell* and *Joe Griffin*, which describes that we are born with evolved needs that seek satisfaction from our environment. (6) Garyl Fuchs of Warwickshire stated that life is the eternal and unbroken flow of infinite, ripping simultaneous events that by a fortuitous chain has led to this universe of elements we are all suspended in, which has somehow led to this present experience of sentient existence. (7) Courtney Walsh of Hampshire asserted Webster's definition "the sequence of physical and mental experiences that make up the existence of an individual" (8) Sheryl Anderson of Illinois restated Shakespeare's interesting ideas about the nature of life in *Macbeth* (Act V, Scene V); and observed that in 5 concise and poetic lines, Shakespeare defined life as an impermanent, non-self-directed, unsatisfactory, limited, ever-changing, and ultimately insignificant code.

(9) …Hall of New Mexico explained that life is the realization of its own contingency, including constant process of becoming, creating value and meaning, accepting finitude such as responsibilities, human existence; which are neither

fixed nor absolute, ambiguous, possibilities entailed existence, conscious of humanity, sadness such as death, suffering, and destruction; happiness such as joy and creativity; finding cause to survive, a reason not to die; can be youth, old age, and everything in between. He concluded that life is beautiful because human life is love and hate but it can only be life when we are with others; as a result, life as fear and hatred is not real at all; and (10) Greg Chatterton of Fife categorically stated that "My life is a mission to help other sufferers"

The Meaning of Life

The concept of positive life regarding an individual's belief that he is fulfilling his positive valued life-framework or life-goal is introduced as an initial definition of meaning in life (Battista, & Almond, 1973, pp.409-427). As a result, the concept of positive life is put forward as providing a reliable and verifiable preliminary operational definition of a meaningful life. (Battista, & Almond, 1973, pp.409-427). However, one reason for the lack of systematic answers given to the question of life's meaning is surely that, as *Updike* notes, this question is imprecise and unclear (Metz, 2001, pp.137-153).

I asked the question: *Is life what we make of it?* Denning (February 2011) argues that life can be what we all make of it; and suggested that the greatest contribution an anthropological perspective can make to this discussion may be in helping us go beyond the attempts at prediction and policy-making such as helping us to look at the biggest picture of the culture within which we live and work. Thus, helping us recognize and question the stories about new life and about contact that are so imbued within our culture that we forget how much we live by them (Denning, February 2011). As a result, helping us to remember that Western scientists share this world with myriad other human beings who think differently and whose voices also matter (Denning, February 2011).

The Philosophical Meaning of Life

Jeffrey and Shackelford (2015) observed that: (a) life is pretty meaningful because in philosophical terms, is broadly construed as an underlying quality of aboutness; (b) contrary to popular perception, our lives hold a great deal of meaning since the meaning of life or the meaning of an individual's life is the essential reason for that existence; (c) philosophical debate about meaning should be exploited to generate interest in the topic because most scholars agree that intrinsic meaning is incoherent such that the meaning can only exist to the extent that it is ascribed by observers; and (d) there should be exploitation of the distinction between the widespread perception of meaning and its intrinsic existence (p.571).

Morange and Falk (2012) have asserted that the question: *What is life?* Is absent from the writings of present-day biologists and scientists and the reasons for this absence are metaphysical, epistemological (potentiality of the knowledge of human being study), and historical; however, no one has full answer to this question, yet there are many good reasons to keep posing it (pp.425-438). Nevertheless, answers are no longer sought in the existence of strengths or mechanisms specific to life (Morange & Falk, 2012, pp.425-438); yet Repp (2018) posited that philosophers once dismissed questions about meaning of life as conceptually confused, because while the talk of life meaning is no longer considered nonsense, most theorist continue to assume that such talk has nothing to do with meaning in the *sign* sense that applies to language (pp.403-427).

The philosophical definitions of life revolve around the views of philosophers (such as Plato, Aristotle, Epicurus, and many more); as well as major teachings of religions (such as Hinduism and Islam). *First,* **Plato** (born 428/427 BCE, Athens, Greece; died 348/347, Athens), ancient *Greek* philosopher; a student of *Socrates* (*c.* 470–399 BCE), teacher of *Aristotle* (384–322 BCE), and founder of *the Academy,* which became known as *the author of philosophical works of unparalleled influence.* Tiberius (2013) asserted that there are five different theories of *well-being,* encompassing: (i) *hedonism, (ii), desire-fulfilment, (iii), life-satisfaction, (iv) nature-fulfilment,* and (v*) objective-list theory* (pp.19-38). Against this background, in Platonism, *the meaning of life* is in the attainment of the highest form of knowledge, which is the *Idea* (Form) of the Good from which all good and just things derive utility and value.

Second, **Aristotle-**Per Aristotle, *Happiness is the ultimate purpose of human existence* and consists of achievement through the course of a whole lifetime, such as all the good- health, wealth, knowledge, friends, and many more that lead to the perfection of human nature and to the enrichment of human life. Aristotle's most influential work is the **Nicomachean Ethics**, where is a theory of happiness that many people believe today and presented despite being over 2,300 years old. The key question Aristotle addressed in these lectures is: (1) *what is the ultimate purpose of human existence?* (2) *What is that end or goal for which we should direct all of our activities?* The ultimate end should be an act that is self-sufficient and final; or *that which*

9

is always desirable in itself and never for the sake of something else (see also Nicomachean Ethics, 097a30-34). People seek pleasure, wealth, and a good reputation everywhere; yet while each has some value, none can occupy the place of the chief good for which humanity should attain unto.

Lastly, **Epicurus** (341-270 BC) – A philosopher who spoke about the meaning of life and also a pupil of the Platonist Pamphilus of Samo. The main article is: *Epicureanism*, the teaching is focused on the greatest good in seeking modest pleasures to attain tranquility and freedom from fear (ataraxia)-via knowledge, friendship, and virtuous, temperate living; where bodily pain (aponia) is absent through one's knowledge of the workings of the world and of the limits of one's desires. As a consequence, combined freedom from pain and freedom from fear are considered happiness in its highest form. Consequently, the *Epicurean* meaning of life rejects immortality and mysticism; while there is a soul, it is as mortal as the body. However, there is no *afterlife*, but one need not fear death because *death is nothing to us; for that which is dissolved, is without sensation, and that which lacks sensation is nothing to us* (Russel, 1946).

Some Religious Beliefs about Life

There are as many beliefs in the meaning of life as there are religions. The beliefs of two major religions will be discussed in the section of the book. **Hinduism-** In all Schools of Hinduism, the meaning of life is tied up to the concepts of *karma* (causal action), *sansara* (the cycle of birth and rebirth), and *moksha* (liberation). Additionally, existence is conceived as the progression of the *ātman* (similar to the western concept of a soul), and its ultimate progression towards liberation from *karma*. As a result, particular goals for life are generally subsumed under broader *yogas* (practices), or *dharma* (correct living); which are intended to create more favorable reincarnations. Though, generally positive acts in this life; yet the goal are to realize the fundamental truth about oneself. For this reason, this thought is conveyed in the *Mahāvākyas* or *Tat Tvam Asi* (thou art that), *Aham Brahmāsmi, Prajñānam Brahma* and *Ayam Ātmā Brahma* (the soul and the world are one-Hopkins, 1971, p. 78).

Islam-The Qur'an describes the purpose of creation as follows: *"Blessed be he in whose hand is the kingdom, he is powerful over all things, who created death and life that he might examine which of you is best in deeds, and he is the almighty, the forgiving"* (Qur'an 67:1–2) and *"And I (Allâh) created not the jinn and mankind except that they should be obedient (to Allah)"* (Qur'an 51:56). Islam acknowledges that the existence of a creator is the first step in understanding the true purpose of life and that God sends guidance through the prophets and the Qur'an; and for this reason, God describes this life as a test and people are tested in different way (Retrieved from islamicpamphlets. com-accessed on 09/26/2019). As a result, the test of one's faith in using one's intellect to contemplate and recognize God's signs to live according to His guidance (Retrieved from islamicpamphlets.com-accessed on 09/26/2019).

The question is: *Can philosophical definitions give the true meaning of life?* There is a bias towards thinking that life has meaning and since this bias has not led to wholesale agreement among philosophers, it seems that something irrational has guided philosophers' answers (Domino, 2012, pp. 363-377). Consequently, Domino (2012) argued that the question of

11

the meaning of life is a by-product of our species' reproductive strategy (pp.363-377). Nevertheless, *Chinese Philosophy* is excluded from the construction of the meaning of life and falls into the dilemma of the life meaning (Deng, 2011, pp. 608-627).

The Bible stipulates in Colossians 2:8: *"Beware lest anyone cheat you through philosophy and empty deceit, according to the tradition of men, according to the basic principles of the world, and not according to Christ" (Emphasis mine)*. Quite apart from the Biblical admonition, some have argued that philosophy is *"the quest for an understanding of the world and man's place in it, and for ways to apply this understanding to the right conduct of life."* While this idea may sound very lofty, any converted Christian knows that the Bible answers the basic questions and many more. Philosophers tend to ask: (a) *Is there a God?* and (b) *how can we distinguish good from bad?* The Word of God gives full and satisfying responses to these queries. As a result, there is no need for a *quest* through the labyrinth of man's mind to find the answers to the questions.

God is not in the knowledge of philosophy; essentially philosophy is a Western practice, with ancient Greece as its originator. In 2015, Harney postulated that phenomenology had a problematic relationship with empirical science; suggesting antipathy to science and to its methods of explaining the natural world (pp.661-669). In the Eastern countries, including ancient Israel and Judah, the search for wisdom related to religious practice. Comparatively, in Israel, thought went from God to life; yet in Greece, thought proceeded from life to God. By way of illustration, God reveals that life is in the blood (Genesis 9:4; Leviticus 17:11), which is true both physically and spiritually. A Christian uses this foundational truth to proceed to understand related things such as observing the presence of oxygen in the blood. God's Word is the foundation of all knowledge; explaining how the human lungs work to inhale oxygen and exhale carbon dioxide, as well as, the circulation of the blood to deliver nutrients to all parts of the body.

Conversely, the Greek philosophers start without the benefit of God's knowledge, utilizing trial and error approaches to arrive at conclusions. For instance, **Thales**, an early Greek philosopher, determined that *water* was the source of life. People listened and accepted-"Wow!" Then, came along another philosopher, who rejected water as the source of life and offered *air* as the source of life. Again, people said-"Wow!" and dropped ignorant Thales. Likewise, **Diogenes**, a seeker of *truth,* rocked the Greek world with his deductions. Diogenes came to the conclusion that *air had intelligence*, and as you might expect, everyone said, "Wow!"

Legend says that during the day he wandered the streets of Athens with a lantern. When asked why, he said he was searching for an honest man. Nevertheless, he and his father had been expelled from Asia Minor for counterfeiting (Retrieved from www.webwinds.com- accessed on 09/26/2019); no doubt he needed help in finding an honest man! In studying the history of philosophy, one observation stands out- Each generation brought new Schools of thought about the meaning of life and related issues. Consequently, no truth is fixed or permanent, but the only constant is change. Thus, there are dozens of contradictory branches of philosophy, encompassing: *Existentialism, Gnosticism, Metaphysics, Platonism, Buddhism, Confucianism, Taoism, Pantheism, Pragmatism, Sophistry, Stoicism, Theosophy*, and *many more.*

The implication is not that thinking is bad but human thoughts must start from the right place. If thinking begins with the foundation of God's truth and continually draws on the Bible as a check to verify whether the thoughts and ideas are grounded, the problems associated with human thoughts will be avoided. Purves and Delon (2018) argued for two *thesis* about the meaning of life: (1) that the best account of meaningful lives must take intentional action to be necessary for meaning because an individual's life has meaning if and only if the individual acts intentionally in ways that contribute to…valuable states of affairs; and (2) that life first *thesis* does not entail that only human lives are meaningful (pp.317-338). The question is: *Are animals' lives meaningful?* If so, why? and how?

I contend that the extrapolation of the meaning of life from the Bible is not philosophy. In fact, *Christian philosophy* may be a contradiction in terms. Kumaran (2018) elaborated that there is an invisible element that is always present in the entire process of creation; as a result, the poet delves deep into the inner recesses of human mind and brings out the presence of the infinite in the thought process and in the human action (pp.16-25). Solomon's wisdom exceeded that of all people (I Kings 4:30), and he became famous in all the surrounding nations for his wisdom (verses 31-34). The question to pose is: (i) *was Solomon a philosopher?* (ii) *Did he pursue wisdom by intellectual means?* (iii) *Did he inquire into the nature of things based on man's logical reasoning rather than observing or experimenting?* Biblical perspectives of life will be explored in subsequent Chapters of this book.

CHAPTER TWO

THE CONCEPT OF LIFE

•

"Ecclesiastes must be read as God's wisdom literature because it is wisdom literature."

— (O'DONNELL, 2014, P.4)

The day- to- day struggles and triumphs are experienced by every creature on this earth. As human beings, we are prone to challenges and confronted with daily decisions. The good news however is that, no matter what issue you're confronted with, you have the freedom to choose how to react. It is essential to note therefore, that, every decision that you make leads us down a path, either for better or for worse. Consequently, every decision you make has significance, leading to the determination of what your life will amount to.

Once a young man asked his father: *what life is?* The father threw the question back at him and asked, *what do you think it is?* This young man begun pouring his heart out- life is difficult, irrational, and very complicated. The father enquired, quite surprised at his son's response. Why those responses?

Well, I don't understand why right from childhood, I will be made to go to school, study difficult subjects, and compete with people who are more intelligent than me. I don't understand why I have to study continuously before I can pass an examination and even when I pass, I have to be constantly upgrading myself and become the best and smart student before any organization would even think of hiring me.

I don't even understand why people have to strive and struggle to make it in life while many successful people I have gotten closer to, seem unhappy and still discontented. So, what's the point in living, struggling to make it in life when in the end that success I'm striving for won't even guarantee me the fulfilment I'm looking for? Not to talk of the fact that one day, I'll have to leave all I've worked for behind and be buried without them.

Daddy, the young man continued, see how wealthy you are, we don't lack anything because you've worked really hard to ensure your children lack nothing, but see how unhappy we all are because we keep battling with one disease or the other. As I'm speaking now, Mama is dying of cancer, and the money you have accrued cannot save her, so tell me how best I should define life. I do not understand why we are born anyway, if in the end we will have to die disgustingly, the young man spouted. At that, the father began to weep uncontrollably such that the young man had to try to console the dad, and ended up weeping too.

That is a sad one, but is that all there is to life? Because, seriously, if what this young man described above is the true meaning of life; then I will join in the charade to announce that life is after all not worth living.

I have come across many people of all classes who still do not know what life truly is. In trying to define life, people give all sorts of weird definitions and meaning. Some of the most intelligent and highly educated of men believe in evolution. Evolution operates on blind chance. That is its fundamental principle. It is the totally fortuitous coming together of just the right elements at just the right time that not only sets off a chain of events that result in life, but also sets off all the processes that resulted in all the forms of life in a continuous stream of fortuitous events.

The theory of evolution states that life is accidental; it is called natural selection. That is its fundamental principle. You take that theory into the area of social circumstances; yet people do not know it, but are being taught that there is neither a *Great Hand* guiding the outcome of this creation, nor who brought creation to being at the beginning. But rather, you see life as accidental, and all of the things that spawn from that are also accidental. This theory contemplates that life, which is far more complicated than a watch or a computer, just happened accidentally! Arguably, if this is what you believe, then life becomes meaningless.

God Defines Life

God's Word establishes a far different foundation for the concept of life. It is a foundation with a purpose. Let us turn to the real beginning of life, found in the Bible in John 1.

> *In the beginning was the Word, and the Word was with God, and the Word was God. He was in the beginning with God. All things were made through Him, and*

17

without Him nothing was made that was made. In
Him was life, and the life was the light of men. And the
light shines in the darkness, and the darkness did not
comprehend it (John 1:1-5)

What the Bible is revealing here is that there is a purposeful creation made by God. The Word was with God, and the Word was also God; Two personalities, yet one God (Jesus and the Father). This Jesus who was with God, had life in Him and all things were created through Him. So, life existing in their creation is something gifted to us from an already subsisting life; as a result, mankind and all the other parts of creation that are alive, have life because God breathed life into them. He did it *purposefully*. It was *not* accidental. He set His *mind* and *will* to give life, and things began to happen.

It was not something He was obligated to do, but rather He was constrained to give life to His creation because He wanted to share what He is with what He has created. That is the purpose behind everything that is made, as we will see as this unfolds in the pages of this book; it is so simple in its logic, that what motivated this creation was the love of God; where He wanted to share what He is, what He is able to do, and with what He makes. He had to give life because He *is* life.

These verses do not explain the purpose of life, but John is laying the foundation for teaching that life, which imparted life, became flesh, and was the light of men. That is, it opened up to mankind this life that was lived; it opened up to mankind by enabling mankind to, first of all, view life through their own lenses, and later on be able to read about it and understand what this life did. Jesus gave life-in *shape* and *form*, as well as, direction to life; which enabled mankind to

18

perceive what is around us; why things were there; and where it was heading towards.

Tan (2016) asserts that empirical evidence confirms the validity of the reconstructed theology regarding the meaning of life in real life experiences. Now, let us turn to Genesis 1. We will again look at these simple principles that are the models for God's great purpose.

Then God said, "Let Us make man in Our image, according to Our likeness; let them have dominion over the fish of the sea, over the birds of the air, and over the cattle, over all the earth and over every creeping thing that creeps on the earth. So, God created man in His own image; male and female He created them (Genesis 1:26-27)

This is the earliest indication we have from God's revelation of the purpose of creation. Mankind is created in the very image of the *One* performing the creation! It implies very strongly in context that, *human life is of immeasurable value;* we are not created after the animal kinds or any other thing, but we are created after the *God-kind*. That is a conclusion that can be reached very easily. Furthermore, God from eternity past had planned that we should be like Him, however, in limited capacity. God planned that man will be a repository of His presence and image. God did not just declare His intention, he actually followed through as a workman generally follows out the motive with which he starts his toil. This did not come by man's effort but, it was God's own idea which by His initiative and power came to pass, and God did this for His own glory and pleasure.

Tan (2016) found that undergirding this framework is the distinctive teaching on the concepts of the worthwhile purpose of life; as well as, coherence in life in appreciating the meaning of life. For this reason, two scriptural references can be provided to support the purpose of God: One, *".......... Him who works all things according to the counsel of His will, that we who first trusted in Christ should be to the praise of His glory"* (Ephesians 1:11-12); and two, *"Everyone who is called by My name, Whom I have created for My glory; I have formed him, yes, I have made him"* (Isaiah 43:7).

Created in the Image Of God

Theologians have explained the image of God in human beings to mean that: *man has the ability for making moral decisions or choices, exhibiting moral purity, possessing intellectual ability or reasoning, taking dominion over the earth, having spiritual nature, and possessing the capacity for immortality.*

Basically, being in the image of God meant that, man was like God in character and represented God on earth. Additionally, the fact that God created human beings for his own glory means that we must fulfil his desire, which is, to glorify him in our lives. This begins with knowing God, submitting to His authority and allowing His presence to be active in us so that we will be delighted in exhibiting the excellence of his character, in whatever we do. We are therefore to do all things to the glory of God (1 Corinthians 10:31).

Created to have Dominion

We find that not only is mankind created in the image of God, but that a major part of the purpose of the creation of mankind is to rule—to have dominion or authority. This is critical to God's purpose, and He said, "*Let them have dominion . . .*" As you can see, God is laying down a foundation for us to understand the path that we are to follow, and it is going to have something to do with God-likeness, and ruling other things. As we begin to have the other pieces together, the conclusion becomes very obvious.

Created for Stewardship

Let us move on to Chapter 2 and we will see that, as God begins to expand the interpretation for dominion, and to be totally and completely of the God-kind, He added *tending and keeping, as follows: "Then the LORD God took the man and put him in the garden of Eden to tend and keep it*" (Genesis 2:15). The environment that God gave to mankind for two people at the time was equipped to serve God's purpose for mankind to allow for the beginning of exercising dominion and creativity in embellishing and preserving that environment from deterioration.

While *tending* means embellishing, cultivating, and decorating; *keeping* means guarding from deterioration. It begins to reach out to those small areas of life, things we might not consider to be very important, but it has to do with how we take care of the things God gives us for our life—whether our bodies, our environment, our homes, our automobiles, and so on. All-in-all, we are here as stewards. Likewise, whether it has to do with the building of character, or the ownership and maintenance of our material things- we are to dress and keep them.

Let us understand that, the universe is a divine gift to man. It was designed by God for the occupation of man. From its

21

highest manifestations to its lowest, is the purpose to minister to man's happiness and needs. Now, it is important to note that, scientific research has provided insights to man to see the richness of the creator's gift to man. Consequently, the purpose of all these is to manifest God's love towards humanity, through- the sun, the moon, the stars, and ultimately, the creation of man are all but a token of God's love.

God has put man in charge of all these to be a steward, for which reason, we are created in His image. We should know God, obey Him, and recognize Him as the source and ultimate owner of all things and to use whatever He has placed at our disposal for His glory. This is fundamental to understanding the meaning of life. But is this how we all view life?

King Solomon

King Solomon; the author of Ecclesiastes who writes about our lives that are 'in this world', uses phrases or words that means 'a breath' or 'wind' to describe life. In reflecting on the true meaning of life, he considers life also as 'a mystery' or 'something that is difficult to understand'. I believe most people share in Solomon's sentiments.

The Book of Ecclesiastes is almost like an autobiography of his own life and includes all of the frustrations of life, the futility of love, and the conclusion of all things here on earth.

The reign of King David and his son, King Solomon, was the golden age of Israel. David's military prowess had relieved his kingdom from the constant threat of foreign invasion, and had established an empire over the surrounding region. Subsequently, his son's diplomatic skills sustained this empire without the need for further war.

Solomon was a youth when he became king. As a young man, he loved the Lord, and he followed the good advice that his father, David gave him. When David was on his *death* bed, he instructed his son Solomon, saying:

I'm about to leave this world. Be strong and mature. Fulfil your duty to the Lord your God. Obey his directions, laws, commands, rules, and written instructions as they are recorded in Moses' Teachings. Then you'll succeed in everything you do wherever you may go. You'll succeed because the Lord will keep the promise, he made to me: 'If your descendants are faithful to me with all their hearts and lives, you will never fail to have an heir on the throne of Israel (1 Kings 2:1-4).

Wow! What a treasure a father can leave his child. Solomon followed the instructions of his father in his early stages of life. He so loved the Lord that he made a lot of sacrifices to the Lord. It is not surprising that the Lord did not permit David to build Him a temple; instead, told him that He wanted David's son- Solomon- to rather build for Him a Temple (1 Kings 6). You can see that the feeling was mutual. The Lord equally loved Solomon unconditionally.

Abraham Lincoln rightly puts it*:* *"Nearly all men can stand adversity, but if you want to test a man's character, give him power"*. Yes, a person's real character is revealed when you test him with wealth and power. Solomon's ways pleased the Lord and so the Lord decided to bless him. One night, the Lord appeared to Solomon in a dream and says to him: *'Solomon, what would you like me to give you?'* (1 Kings 3:4, 5). Let's see the conversation that ensued between the Lord and Solomon in the dream:

23

Solomon answered, "You have shown great kindness to your servant, my father David, because he was faithful to you and righteous and upright in heart. You have continued this great kindness to him and have given him a son to sit on his throne this very day. "Now, Lord my God, you have made your servant king in f ace of my father David. But I am only a little child nd do not know how to carry out my duties. Your ser vant is here among the people you have chosen, a great people, too numerous to count or number. So, give your servant a discerning heart to govern your people and to distinguish between right and wrong. For who is able to govern this great people of yours? (1Kings 3: 6-11).

God offered Solomon the chance to ask for anything he wanted. Disregarding the things, a king might want, such as wealth, respect, security, health among other things some of us in our days will ask from the Lord; Solomon asked instead for wisdom so he could carry out the responsibilities God had given him. *Is n't that fascinating? How many in our days, given this opportunity, will first consider the welfare of others above our own?* The majority of us will rather opt for the pleasures of the world that will make us more comfortable or powerful to subdue our enemies but Solomon did no such a thing.

In seeking to be a great King who will rule over his nation better, he requested for wisdom. That was a sensible choice he made, considering the fact that with wisdom, one can acquire all that one wanted. Solomon saw that wisdom was a *'need'* and decided to go for it rather than going for a *'want'*. Since he was probably only about 20 years of age, he readily admitted to his lack of qualification and experience to be king in the first place (1 Chronicles 22:5; 29:1).

Of course, wealth, fame, prestige and all the other things I mentioned early on are equally important, but those were not Solomon's priority at that crucial time of his reign. God was pleased with this request, and gave Solomon the great wisdom he requested of Him. But quite amazingly, the Lord did not only grant Solomon his request, but also added both wealth and honour to his prayer:

> *So, God said to him, "Since you have asked for this and not for long life or wealth for yourself, nor have asked for the death of your enemies but for discernment in administering justice, I will do what you have asked. I will give you a wise and discerning heart, so that there will never have been anyone like you, nor will there ever be. Moreover, I will give you what you have not asked for both wealth and honor so that in your lifetime you will have no equal among kings (1 Kings 3:11-13).*

God gave Solomon the great wisdom He had promised him, and Solomon's fame spread throughout the region. This story reminds me of Jesus' discussion and advise to His disciples in Matthew 6:33 that: *"But seek first his kingdom and his righteousness, and all these things will be given to you as well"* (Matthew 6:33). Jesus, earlier on in the Chapter had just told His followers not to worry about material things such as food or clothing, as the Lord will provide the needs of His followers. This meant that, Jesus required of all His followers not to pursue wealth and material things before *the things of the Lord*. This verse, like the scenario in Solomon's request ties in the two notions together; if one places the pursuit of the Kingdom of God first; then, material needs will automatically follow with no need for anxiety or worry.

King Solomon's Wealth

While the Bible does not assign a value or weight to all the silver, bronze, precious gems, garments, spices, among others that Solomon possessed, it does give us a rough estimation of how much gold he brought in and how rich he was. For example, every year, King Solomon received over twenty-five (25) tons (other translations say six hundred and sixty-six (666) talents of gold, in addition to the taxes paid by merchants (1Kings 10:14 - 15).

A talent was an ancient unit of measurement for weighing precious metals, usually, gold and silver. A talent weighs roughly 75 pounds or 34.3 kilograms, which is equal to 1,094 troy ounces. At *$1,500* per troy ounce, a talent of gold in today's value is worth *$1,641,000*. At *$1,600* per troy ounce, a talent is worth *$1,750,400*. If Solomon received 666 talents of the metal each year; then, this means the value of what he got each year was between US*$1,092,906,000* and US*$1,165,766,400* U.S. dollars. Incredible!

Using Google search for the computation of the networth of Solomon, I tried to find the value of his gold as recorded in 1Kings 10, in today's currency. The consecutive networth of King Solomon is estimated at US$2.1 trillion (Retrieved from https://www.quora.com/What-is-the-estimate-of-king-solomons-wealth-in-todays-economy-and-is-he-the-likely-richest-accessed on 08/17/2019).

The Bible describes King Solomon's networth as: "*that dwarfed any and every person who lived before him, making him the wealthiest person in the world*". The calculation is based on the assumptions below:

First, per the Biblical history, the reign of King Solomon spanned from 970 BC to 931 BC (Retrieved from https://www.quora.com/What-is-the-estimate-of-king-solomons-wealth-in-todays-economy-and-is-he-the-likely-richest-accessed on 08/17/2019).

Second, King Solomon reigned for about 40 years and he received 25 tons of gold each year, which could be trillions of dollars (Retrieved from https://www.quora.com/What-is-the-estimate-of-king-solomons-wealth-in-todays-economy-and-is-he-the-likely-richest-accessed on 08/17/2019).

Three, one (1) ton of Gold is worth *$64.3 Million dollars at $2000/oz* (Google search-on 08/17/2019).

Four, if one (1) ton of Gold is worth $64.3 Million dollars at $2000/oz; then, 25 tons times 40 years of reign amounts to *$64,300,800,000 (*Retrieved from https://www.quora.com /What-is-the-estimate-of-king-solomons-wealth-in-todays-economy-and-is-he-the-likely-richest-accessed on 08/17/2019*)*. However, this number does not include incomes derived from *trade, business, and vocation*; as well as, the annual tribute paid by subjects, including governors and kings of Arabia (Retrieved from https://www.quora.com/What-is-the-estimate-of-king-solomons-wealth-in-todays-economy-and-is-he-the-likely-richest-accessed on 08/17/2019).

Five, pure gold and ivory were used to decorate King Solomon's throne, which had 6 stairs and 12 lion statues on either side along each step and grounded on a solid foot stool of gold; where, two larger lion statues stood on the sides of the throne (Retrieved from https://www.quora.com/ What-is-the-estimate-of-king-solomons-wealth-in-todays-economy-and-is-he-the-likely-richest-accessed on 08/17/2019).

Six, the household articles and goblets in Solomon's palace were of pure gold. Consequently, King Solomon was reported as very rich during his reign in Jerusalem, which caused his immense wealth in silver to be viewed as of little value, just as rocks. As a result, nothing in his palace was made of silver (Retrieved from https://www.quora.com/What-is-the-estimate-of-king-solomons-wealth-in-todays-economy-and-is-he-the-likely-richest-accessed on 08/17/2019).

Solomon became immensely wealthy that all his cups were made of gold (1Kings 10: 21). His wealth was so vast that gold and silver were as common in Jerusalem as stones (2 Chronicles 1:15; 1Kings 10: 27), and all these are as a result of one good choice he made- *to place the needs of God and the people of the Lord first.* Life consist of a series of experiences, some bad, others good. But really, life involves the totality of activities, actions, choices among others that make up our experiences while living on earth. Thus, we are the entirety of experiences that we encounter as we go through life.

Everyone wants to find happiness and fulfilment in life. No matter our circumstances. The search for true satisfaction is at the heart of everyone's goals. Yet, the choice to be happy and fulfilled has been given to you but others still struggle to find it because they're looking for the right answers at the wrong places. You see, for some people, just like the young man whose story I narrated early on in this chapter, they only believe life is all about having the capacity to grow, reproduce, striving to be successful, and gradually change to become old and finally die. Such people see life as a continuous and

28

reoccurring cycle where one is born, grows, go to school to acquire some accolades, marry and give birth, raise kids to also go through the same cycle. Such a life will be frustrating and truly boring.

Life is the most important thing man has at his disposal. Without life, you can't do anything and that's the reason the moment you die, you're carried away into a place far from the living. No matter how prominent or influential one may be, after death, all your prestige, wealth, and goals become irrelevant as they all return with you into the grave, where the dead belongs. To live is the key. Trust me, there are a lot of successful people in the grave now that would happily give up all their successes and wealth to be alive just for one more day so they could make one more decision right and then go back to the grave.

Solomon chose wisdom over riches and God added unto him riches, prestige, and fame such that in all his generation, no one could measure up to his great insight and wealth. In his lifetime, he enjoyed peace and prosperity. This tells us that life is full of choices and each choice has a consequence attached to it. *What kind of things do you pray for? Do you believe those things are what life is all about?*

CHAPTER THREE

CHOICES BECOME LIFE

•

Man has been created as a free moral agent and must make the choice either to live a happy, fulfilled life, or a life full of frustrations. Going back to Genesis Chapter 2, God gave man the liberty to enjoy life but with certain restrictions; He instructed man not to eat from the tree of the knowledge of good and evil.

From this biblical account, I see that right at the doorstep of human existence, God places choices at the doorsteps of man: first, *"The LORD God planted a Garden eastward in Eden, and there He put the man whom He had formed. And out of the ground the LORD God made every tree grow that is pleasant to the sight and good for food. The tree of life was also in the midst of the garden, and the tree of the knowledge of good and evil."* (Genesis 2:8-9). Second, *"Then the LORD God took the man and put him in the Garden of Eden to tend and keep it. And the LORD God commanded the man, saying, "Of every tree of the Garden you may freely eat; but of the tree of the knowledge of good and evil you shall not eat, for in the day that you eat of it you shall surely* die" (Genesis 2:15-17). Have you ever struggled to make a very difficult decision? The truth is that most decisions seem innocent from the beginning but they all have consequences no matter how small or insignificant you think that decision may be.

I've never come across anyone who deliberately set goals with the aim of becoming a failure, a drug addict, alcoholic, womanizer, a school dropout, or gamble their savings away, or becoming emotionally-chained and miserable in life. These things usually happen as a result of some bad choices people make; however, they turn to blame it on God. Many peoples' anger towards God has been exemplified in: (i) lower religiosity, (ii) more depressive symptoms, (iii) more difficult in finding meaning, and (iv) belief that greater pain is being experienced (Exline, Prince-Paul, Root, & Peereboom, 2013, p.369).

It always begins as though it's no big deal, like getting emotionally-involved with a non-believer of your Christian faith; even though, you know that is not the best. Also, it could be a peak at something you know wasn't meant for your eyes to behold, among other things.

The story in Genesis reveals that man instead of choosing to live a fulfilled life by obeying God, rather choose to go against God's Word and incurred upon himself a life full of toil, frustrations, sorrows, fear, and even death. *How did this happen?* The Bible states:

> *Then to Adam He said, "Because you have heeded the voice of your wife, and have eaten from the tree of which I commanded you, saying, 'You shall not eat of it':*

"Cursed is the ground for your sake; in toil you shall eat of it All the days of your life. Both thorns and thistles it shall bring forth for you, and you shall eat the herb of the field. In the sweat of your face you shall eat bread till you return to the ground, for out of it you were taken; For dust you are, and to dust you shall return (Genesis 3:17-19)

Do you see what is going on here? In Genesis 2:15-17, God had given mankind the freedom to eat of any tree in the *Garden* including the *tree of life*, but forbids them from eating of the *tree of knowledge of good and evil*. God added that, they will die if they ate it. Following through the story, you will see that, they decided to rebel against God by eating of the tree of knowledge of good and evil; even though, they had been forewarned of the repercussions. Well, one may say: the devil tempted them. Yes, they were tempted but they were not forced. What they did was not something against their will; it was their own decision; hence, God could not exonerate them from the consequences of their actions. *"No one has power over you unless you give it to them, you are in control of your life and your choices decide your own fate"*- *Leon Brown* (Retrieved from https://livelifehappy.com/life-quotes/no-one-has-power-over-you-accessed on 08/17/2019).

As humans, we have the tendency to display some innocent disregard for the bigger picture, which are the consequences that will follow the choices we make and actions we take. Suffice it to say, life doesn't just happen. Instead, our lives are defined by the choices we make. Some of these choices are made by us, while some are made by other people, and we just accept those decisions and follow along. Sometimes, either you or someone

32

around you choose what the next thought, or the next step, or action should be. Whether you consent to these choices or not, your development as an individual follow the choices that guide or influence your life.

You see, day in and day out, you'll be confronted with issues, but the choice is yours to make. I love this Hebrew young man- Joseph. He never took life for granted. He knew he had a great destiny and was willing to do anything possible to protect that destiny. Joseph, who was a slave in Egypt, pleased his master-Potiphar, and so, his master entrusted everything in his household into his care. But then, Joseph's good-looking and calmly nature caught the attention of his master's wife and she commanded Joseph to commit adultery with her.

Joseph refused, explaining that this would be an affront to his master (Potiphar) and a sin to his God. However, when it became obvious that Potiphar's wife was unrelenting and determined to carry on with her evil intentions, Joseph fled. When matters became worse, he didn't wait to negotiate things with the evil woman, whose mind was made up (Genesis 39). He fled from her presence. Additionally, Joseph perceived that sleeping with his master's wife could destroy the glorious destiny and beautiful life the Lord had in store for him. Therefore, he made a choice, and as a result of that choice, he lived that life the Lord had destined for him. Through him, his entire lineage and all the Egyptians were saved from famine (Genesis 45).

In the early life of Solomon, we see a promising young zealous believer for the Lord, who became richer and wiser than all the Kings in his region. You saw how he was determined to follow his father's instructions of pleasing the Lord in all his ways.

As a result, the Lord blessed him mightily. I'm sure Solomon's lifestyle and wealth was enviable to most people.

We listen to the story of Solomon and we're excited about the fact that, he was successful, wise, and influential. We tend to believe that life is all about accumulating all the wealth in the world, becoming successful, living extravagantly, and many more. In the book of Ecclesiastes, Solomon reflects on life in relation to long years of experience but short on lasting rewards.

As king, Solomon had the opportunity and resources to pursue the rewards of righteousness, wisdom, pleasure, and work. Nevertheless, the world-weary tone of his writing in the book of Ecclesiastes suggests that late in life, he looked back on his choices with regret. Under Solomon's reign, Israel reached her utmost peak as a nation; including honour, wealth, prestige, fame, and power. The splendour and skilful administration of the greatest kingdom.

Sadly though, at the end of Solomon's reign, Israel had become temporarily and spiritually bankrupt, leading to deterioration and contention everywhere. Just within only a year of Solomon's death, the land was divided into two kingdoms, and the course of Israel's history was permanently altered.

Solomon made some really bad choices and decisions that changed the course of Israel's history and became part of his life forever. Like it's mostly said, *"it's not how you start that's important, but how you finish!"*- Jim George (Retrieved from https://www.goodreads.com/ author/ quotes/ 17561. Jim_George?page=3-accessed on 08/17/2019). *What actions or events led to the nation's dramatic fall from grace to grass?* Solomon undoubtedly started strong but then along the line, we see him faltering. For example, very early in his reign, it is reported that he married Pharaoh's daughter, a political marriage. Probably, he married her to cease the contention between Israel and Egypt. But the question is: *Was it the right thing to do, or was it the will of God for him to marry from Egypt?* Couldn't the Lord have provided the desired security and well-deserved peace in Israel under his reign? Keep in mind that the Lord had explicitly told the people of Israel not to marry daughters of foreign kings or women from foreign nations. To this end, he turned his back on the Lord the very minute he defiled His orders.

In I Kings Chapter 11, starting at verse 1, we read:

> *Now King Solomon loved many foreign women along with the daughter of Pharaoh, Moabite, Ammonite, Edomite, Sedonian, and Hittite women from the nations concerning which the Lord had said to the people of Israel, 'You shall not enter into marriage with them, neither shall they with you, for surely they will turn away your hearts after their gods.'" Solomon clung to these women in love. He had 700 wives, princesses, and 300 concubines and his wives turned his heart after other gods, and his heart was not truly whole to the Lord his God as was the heart of David, his father*

The text goes on to talk about Solomon building temples to all these foreign gods. How sad! *"Solomon built such shrines for all his foreign wives to use for burning incense and sacrificing to their gods"- 1 Kings 11:8.* To add to this, Solomon employed forced labour, coupled with excessive taxation to finance his massive building projects.

During the reign of Rehoboam, son of Solomon and following Solomon's death, the ten northern tribes appealed for relief from the heavy tax burden, but Rehoboam refused. The Israelites returned home in rebellious anger, and later assassinated him (1 Kings 12).

And as you read carefully, the first eleven chapters in I Kings, you see Solomon's life going downhill. Eventually, the wisest man becomes fool per his own language. Had it not been for David's faithfulness to the Lord, Solomon's lineage will never have had any inheritance in the kingdom again.

In spite of the great legacy from David, wisdom from God, the affluence, and security that characterized his early life, Solomon fell away from the Lord and lived a life full of sin and reproach. As a consequence, the heydays of Israel were short-lived. As soon as Solomon died, the kingdom was split, with Solomon's heir, Rehoboam retaining the smaller portion. These split kingdoms experienced much trouble that resulted from Solomon's sins and bad choices. Quite a life of the world's wisest man who died a fool. What is the most important factor in determining the outcome of your life?

God has given us the freedom to make choices but His desire is that, we will choose life and good. This is subject to how submissive we are to live in obedience to His word. Reflect on this passage of scripture:

> *See, I set before you today life and prosperity, death and destruction. For I command you today to love the LORD your God, to walk in obedience to him, and to keep his commands, decrees and laws; then you will live and increase, and the LORD your God will bless you in*

the land you are entering to possess. But if your heart turns away and you are not obedient, and if you are drawn away to bow down to other gods and worship them, I declare to you this day that you will certainly be destroyed. You will not live long in the land you are crossing the Jordan to enter and possess. This day I call the heavens and the earth as witnesses against you that I have set before you life and death, blessings and curses. Now choose life, so that you and your children may live and that you may love the LORD your God, listen to his voice, and hold fast to him. For the LORD is your life, and he will give you many years in the land he swore to give to your fathers, Abraham, Isaac and Jacob (Deuteronomy 30:15-20).

CHAPTER FOUR

SUFFERINGS IN LIFE, WHO IS RESPONSIBLE?

•

There is no question that a great deal of evil and suffering is in the world. No matter what you do, or who you are, you are going to experience suffering in some way, shape, or form and this often lead people to wonder whether life is worth living. Some even go to the extent of asking whether a loving God exists. There are dark pieces to the puzzle; they constitute the black border that connects to the dark gray pieces of death, injustice, and other bleak realties (O'Donnell, 2014, p.9). Where was God when I was encountering all those problems? I am a faithful Christian; I pay my tithe, attend services regularly, why has God brought all these calamities upon me?

The question to be posed is: *Is God responsible for every calamity?* The brevity of death and life as natural end of life can create an urgency to live every moment with zeal and vigor, when the probability of the *afterlife* is uncertain (Levicheva, 2014).

Does all those ranting and fuming sound familiar? I won't be surprised if you have even asked God similar questions before.

Nearly everywhere we look, the world seems to be whirling out of control because disasters of all shapes and sizes are progressively altering how we live. We see the herculean storms of global peril. I've seen many people asking and searching for answers to the world's problems. Others have come to believe that life is all about suffering and fighting constant battles. But is that really the case?

In response to this dilemma, Da Silva and Murilo (2016) elaborated, as follows: *first*, suffering has no sense because life itself has none. *Second*. A depressing existence is an external victim of destiny; and as a result, there is the need to confront suffering as a human condition from which there is no escape. *Three*, it is not simple to give in but rather to find one's own way forward through suffering amid misfortune and anguish. Consequently, the existence of suffering and pain in the world has caused many people to question their faith for ages.

The question several people ask is: "*Is God responsible for all the problems in the world?*" If God is Sovereign over all things; then, *why doesn't He stop all those problems from befalling man?* Let us find out who is actually responsible for the sufferings in this world and how we can respond to them in order to make life meaningful.

Sufferings due to the Fall of Mankind, and Nature

In Chapter 1 of this book, we saw how God created a perfect world and gave man authority over it. Our first parents, Adam and Eve rejected all that God had offered them and chose to rebel. Their actions resulted in suffering and death. This is captured as follows:

> *To the woman He said: "I will greatly multiply your sorrow and your conception; In pain you shall bring forth children; Your desire shall be for your husband, and he shall rule over you." Then to Adam He said, "Because you have heeded the voice of your wife, and have eaten from the tree of which I commanded you, saying, 'You shall not eat of it': "Cursed is the ground for your sake; In toil you shall eat of it All the days of your life (Genesis 3:16-19).*

When mankind fell, they moved from the *state of innocence* and entered into a *dispensation of conscience*. So, we read that as soon as they ate the fruit from the tree of knowledge of good and evil, their eyes were opened and they realized that they were naked. Adam's sin of disobedience was a repudiation of God's authority over his life. And this is what sin is all about.

The repercussion of the fall of man encompasses the following:

(1) Now, since the fall of man, we do not find man demonstrating the full image of God as the Bible presents. (2) By nature, we are not fully as God's image as we were meant to be; (3) our moral purity and integrity do not reflect God's holiness; (4) our intellectual ability is faulty, and not glorifying to God. Likewise, (5) Our desire or moral choice is misdirected to personal love; (6) our relationship with God is aimed at personal interests rather than love or God's glory; (7) our relationship with one another is governed by selfishness rather than selflessly serving one another.

Let us consider some few Bible passages here. Please pause here and read the following verses: Romans 1:18-32; 3:10-20; and Psalm 14:1-3). *Did you read them?* If you did not, please stop here and go back to read because they inform us of man's ruined nature and what it produces.

Exline, Prince-Paul, Root, and Peereboom (2013) conducted a survey on the spiritual struggle of anger towards God, using family members of hospice patients and found that 43 percent reported anger and disappointment towards God at low level of intensity (p.369). In fact, this is the verdict – no one is righteous and that, the whole world is guilty before God, judging by His standard, every mouth is stopped. – For instance, let us do a test of ourselves now – have you ever lied? Have you ever hurt or offended somebody by your words or actions? Have you ever become bitter toward a friend? Are you always faithful? Or let me put it this way; do you like everyone else in this world?

I strongly believe that, if you were honest with yourself, you may have answered- Yes! to at least one of the first three questions or No! to one of the last two. So, you see, nobody is righteous before God by his own merits. *All have sinned and come short of the glory of God.* Similarly, *the wages of sin is death* and this might seem like a harsh consequence for sin but we fail to understand the wretchedness of sin compared to God's holiness. God is entirely pure and set apart from evil and in His perfect justice He must punish sin.

Also, in one sense, death is a merciful punishment; can you imagine what it would be like to live forever in a fallen world? Wicked people would never die, and if they knew there were no serious consequences for sin; then, they would act anyway they wanted and the world would become even worse. However, the fact that God allows us to live at all demonstrates His abundant love and mercy. Furthermore, as if that is not enough, He has provided the way for man to be saved from sin and to dwell on this earth with God's peace reigning in his life. Likewise, He has allowed for man to dwell eternally with Him through the sacrificial death and resurrection of His Son, Jesus Christ.

"For all have sinned and fall short of the glory of God, being justified freely by His grace through the redemption that is in Christ Jesus" (Romans 3:23-24). So, you see, *God cannot be responsible*; what He gives is good and perfect. We need to make the right choices to get connected to God and stay connected. Going back to the life of Solomon, we see how God granted Solomon wisdom, fame, and prosperity; and yet, he went ahead to exact monies through taxation from the people of Israelites to finance his massive infrastructural (building) projects.

In the end the people were under intense pressure and going through financial turmoil during his reign. No wonder they pleaded with his immediate successor to reduce the heavy taxes his father- Solomon had imposed on them. I contend that the Israelites under Solomon's rule might have asked a lot of similar questions as to why they were paying a lot of heavy taxes and undergoing financial hardships during the era of their beloved wise king, Solomon.

The question is: *Was God responsible for their hardship.* In our dispensation, the story is not so different. *Is God responsible for all these hardships in our dispensation?* The answer is an emphatic- No! The Book of 1 Samuel 8 reminds us of how the people of Israel demanded that the Prophet Samuel gets them their own king in consonance with what pertains in other nations. Nevertheless, despite the caution about the rulership of human kings, they still went ahead to install Saul as a king.

Now, take a critical look at what transpired between the Lord, the Prophet Samuel, and the people of Israel when Samuel attempted to tell the Israelites that a king will only turn them into slaves instead of uniting them. The people thought that was stupid and ignored Samuel's admonitions. They wanted a king to govern them and fight their battles and God told Samuel to give the people what they wanted and to find them a king (1Samuel 8):

But when they said, "Give us a king to lead us," this displeased Samuel; so, he prayed to the Lord. And the Lord told him: "Listen to all that the people are saying to you; it is not you they have rejected, but they have rejected me as their king. As they have done from the day, I brought them up out of Egypt until this day, forsaking me and serving other gods, so they are doing to you. Now listen to them; but warn them solemnly and let them know what the king who will reign over them will claim as his rights." Samuel told all the words of the Lord to the people who were asking him for a king. He said, "This is what the king who will reign over you will claim as his rights: He will take your sons and make them serve with his chariots and horses, and they will run in front of his chariots. Some he will assign to be commanders of thousands and commanders of fifties, and others to plow his ground and reap his harvest, and still others to make weapons of war and equipment for

*his chariots. He will take your daughters to be perfumers
and cooks and bakers. He will take the best of your fields
and vineyards and olive groves and give them to his
attendants. He will take a tenth of your grain and of
your vintage and give it to his officials and attendants.
Your male and female servants and the best of your
cattle and donkeys he will take for his own use. He
will take a tenth of your flocks, and you yourselves will
become his slaves. When that day comes, you will cry out
for relief from the king you have chosen, but the Lord
will not answer you in that day." But the people refused
to listen to Samuel. "No!" they said. "We want a king
over us. Then we will be like all the other nations, with
a king to lead us and to go out before us and fight our
battles (1 Samuel: 8:6-20).*

Did you carefully read the scriptures above? Then, you'll
notice that the Israelites brought those hardships upon
themselves. So far as we decide to set human beings as rulers
over us then, we should be ready to make allowances for their
imperfections. *Why would you blame life's problems on a perfect
God when He has placed your will in your hands?* Yes, God is
sovereign, but then, He does not impose His will on anyone,
not even Christians. That is the beauty of Christianity. All
of mankind, including God's children have the freewill to
choose what is good from bad and to walk in the right path.
What God does is to guide you through your decisions, and
He can only do that when we allow Him. The God we serve is
a perfect gentleman who would not want to interfere in your
life unless you invite Him to do so.

When God permits Sufferings

The Bible emphatically tells us that God is not responsible for the chaos, negativities, and sufferings among other things that we go through. Looking at the biblical description of God's character and being, He cannot inflict suffering on His people. Yet, in the same Bible, God is sometimes presented as permitting various kinds of sufferings. And when He permits sufferings to come upon a person, it may not be as a result of that person's mistakes or bad choices. I know a man who was described as "blameless and upright", a man who shunned evil, and yet, his life was intertwined with sufferings and calamities which came by God's own permission (Job 1-2). Again, in the New Testament, we are informed of how God permitted Paul to carry in his flesh a thorn, something that the Apostle wished it was not there. Some of these things are difficult to comprehend and can make you feel angry at God. Does this sound familiar? If yes, you are not the first Christian to have felt angry at God. And you will probably not be the last to feel the urge to blame him.

Often, we talk about God testing us and bringing trials into our lives and that we should *"Count it all joy, my brothers, when you meet trials of various kinds, for you know that the testing of your faith produces steadfastness"* (James 1:2, 3). And yet, we need to be cautious as our vision of His sovereignty expands, that we do not attribute something to Him in a way the Scripture does not.

The Apostle James himself, sensing a possible misunderstanding of his powerful statement in James 1, which urges us to count our trials as joy, wants to make sure we know God is not the

45

dispenser of evil in the same way He is the giver of good. He stands sovereignly over both good and evil; however, He stands strictly behind good, and dispassionately, as it were, against evil. Consider what the Lord says in Proverbs 8:13: *"To fear the LORD is to hate evil; I hate pride and arrogance, evil behaviour and perverse speech"* (Proverbs 8:13). Now, *how can such a God who clearly commands His children who fear Him to hate evil be responsible for the very evil things that happen in the world?*

Again, *how on earth could God be reconciled with immense, monstrous evil?* The Apostle James however, gives us an answer to the evil doing in this world. *"When tempted, no one should say, "God is tempting me." For God cannot be tempted by evil, nor does he tempt anyone; but each person is tempted when they are dragged away by their own evil desire and enticed. Then, after desire has conceived, it gives birth to sin; and sin, when it is full-grown, gives birth to death"* (James 1:13-15).

Clearly, God cannot be blamed for your mistakes, selfish desires, and ambitions; neither can He be blamed for the results your covetous life brings upon you or upon this world. When He permits sufferings to come our way, it is always meant for our good. A critical look into the instances of Job and Paul as cited above, they reveal that, God permit us to go through sufferings so we come to better understand our need for and reliance upon God. It is also an opportunity for us to proof the genuineness of our faith (Romans 5:1-5). Satan is put to shame and God is glorified (Job 1:22). Again, God uses the sufferings we go through to perfect, establish, strengthen, and settle and us. *"But may the God of all grace, who called us to His eternal glory by Christ Jesus, after you have suffered a while, perfect, establish, strengthen, and settle you."* (1 Peter 5:10).

Suffering due to the work of Satan

When the Good God is not guiding a country; then, obviously, Satan and his cohorts become rulers. Since, the devil has no good thing in him; you cannot expect the best from him.

Satan is presented as the cause of certain aspects of sufferings; he harnesses the powers of the fallen world to bring hardships to people (2 Thessalonians 2:9-10). He induces spiritual attacks which sometimes, manifest in sufferings, illness and other physical infirmities, even sometimes in death. He is always behind man's disobedience to God (Ephesians 2:2). His goal is always to cause the believer to curse or denounce God and he has only one agenda: kill, steal and destroy (John 10:10). No wonder the Apostle Paul admonishes in the Book of Ephesians to be alert and guarded:

> *Finally, be strong in the Lord and in his mighty power. Put on the full armor of God, so that you can take your stand against the devil's schemes. For our struggle is not against flesh and blood, but against the rulers, against the authorities, against the powers of this dark world and against the spiritual forces of evil in the heavenly realms. Therefore, put on the full armor of God, so that when the day of evil comes, you may be able to stand your ground, and after you have done everything, to stand. Stand firm then, with the belt of truth buckled around your waist, with the breastplate of righteousness in place, and with your feet fitted with the readiness that comes from the gospel of peace. In addition to all this, take up the shield of faith, with which you can extinguish all the flaming arrows of the evil one. Take the helmet of salvation and the sword of the Spirit,*

which is the word of God. And pray in the Spirit on all
occasions with all kinds of prayers and requests. With
this in mind, be alert and always keep on praying for all
the Lord's people (Ephesians 6:10-18).

Dear reader, it is important to understand that, suffering in life is inevitable and no matter the source. What the Christian should know is that, as a child of God, suffering is always for a purpose. We should endeavour to understand it and learn from it (Psalm 119:67). We should also believe that, God cares for us and that, He will not allow Satan to harm us; Satan will not be able to touch the Christian except with God's permission (Job 1:9-10). Finally, God has made us wonderful promises, if we remain faithful to Him, those promises will come to pass in our lives. *What will you choose?*

Effects of the choices we make

From all indications, the Lord made available unto Solomon everything a king would need to have a successful reign. He lacked nothing; wisdom, fame, prestige, riches; because the sovereign Lord Himself was on his side. But what do we see in the later part of his reign on earth? Solomon forsook the instructions of his father, David and instead chose to do the very things that were detestable in the sight of God. Solomon was enticed by his own lustful desires and decided to satisfy those desires regardless how the Lord will feel about his choices. So here, we see that even though the Lord loved Solomon so much, He still could not impose His will on him, because He expects His children to serve Him willingly out of love and not out of fear.

The best the Lord will do is to warn you of the impending danger your decision may bring upon you so that you could turn from your mistakes or wicked ways. One would think that the Lord just looked on and watched Solomon go wayward and destroy his destiny-No! He warned Solomon twice to be careful of his ways and yet, he did not obey Him. *"Even though the Lord, the God of Israel, had appeared to Solomon twice and had commanded him not to worship foreign gods, Solomon did not obey the Lord but turned away from him"* (1 Kings 11:9-10).

You see, like Solomon, most Christians are guilty of similar iniquities. We turn our backs on God and fulfil our own desires without considering the outcome of such actions and decisions. And when things begin to go haywire, we turn to put the blame on God, accusing Him of bringing those problems on us when we started the fire in the first place.

The Lord transferred the kingdom of Israel to Solomon because David, his father, was faithful to the Lord. Out of David's faithfulness, the Lord promised him that if his descendants also remained faithful to Him, then, the kingship would never leave his lineage. However, Solomon destroyed all that with his waywardness. See what happened afterwards:

> *So, the Lord was angry with Solomon and said to him, "Because you have deliberately broken your covenant with me and disobeyed my commands, I promise that I will take the kingdom away from you and give it to one of your officials. However, for the sake of your father David I will not do this in your lifetime, but during the reign of your son. And I will not take the whole*

kingdom away from him; instead, I will leave him one
tribe for the sake of my servant David and for the sake
of Jerusalem, the city I have made my own (1 Kings
11:11-13).

In spite of Solomon's great wisdom and all the peace and provisions he enjoyed from the Lord during his reign he turned to a life of sin. And so, brought a lot of consequences on the very people he longed for wisdom to rule discreetly. Dear reader, you can't turn your back on the Lord and still expect Him to be accountable to you when calamity strikes. We are responsible for the choices we make. God promises to be a God to the country which will trust, fear, seek His will, and obey Him. Almost all the countries in the world have not met this basic requirement, and tend to seek their own ways; thereby, stepping on each other's toes and bringing about wars, sufferings, peril, and many evil consequences on ourselves.

CHAPTER FIVE

THE PROFITABILITY OF LIFE

•

Metz (2015) proffered the meaning that great meaning in life, at least in so far as it comes from this triad, is a matter of positively orienting one's rational nature towards fundamental conditions of human existence, and the conditions of human life responsibilities. *"Meaningless! Meaningless!" says the Teacher. "Utterly meaningless! Everything is meaningless." What do people gain from all their labours at which they toil under the sun?"* (Ecclesiastes 1:1-3).

Based on King Solomon's reflections of life and the vanity of it all, the question of whether or not life is profitable has weighed hard on people, especially, when you become painfully aware that death is lurking at your door and awaiting your escort. I pose the question: *Is Life Profitable?* I can share in the pains, frustration, and confusion of the young man whose story I narrated in the first chapter of this book about how he thought life was not worth living.

His father has worked so hard in his lifetime just so he could secure the future of his family. He wanted his wife and kids to enjoy a comfortable life and be happy; but in the end, after getting the pleasures of the world, such as providing everything his family needed; just like Solomon, they're not content and fulfilled. Like Solomon, the young man told his dad that he doesn't think life was profitable; thinking to himself, my mother is ravaged by a cruel disease and slowly dying and all the money we've accumulated can't save her. He has pretty much lost his youthful enthusiasm already.

Solomon really had his fair share of the pleasures of the world. He was the wisest man who ever lived. Ponder over this: *"Solomon's wisdom was greater than the wisdom of all the people of the East, and greater than all the wisdom of Egypt"* (1 Kings 4:30). Likewise, his wisdom earned him so much respect and fame such that one time the *Queen of Sheba* travelled all the way from her kingdom to Jerusalem to experience at first hand the wisdom of King Solomon. This account is capture as follows:

> *When the queen of Sheba heard about the fame of Solomon and his relationship to the Lord, she came to test Solomon with hard questions. Arriving at Jerusalem with a very great caravan with camels carrying spices, large quantities of gold, and precious stones she came to Solomon and talked with him about all that she had on her mind. Solomon answered all her questions; nothing was too hard for the king to explain to her. When the queen of Sheba saw all the wisdom of Solomon and the palace he had built, the food on his table, the seating of his officials, the attending servants in their robes, his*

*cupbearers, and the burnt offerings he made at the temple
of the Lord, she was overwhelmed (1 Kings 10:1-5).*

The wisdom and prosperity of Solomon was truly
overwhelming. Read the Queen of Sheba's perspectives
regarding Solomon after she was awed by what happened in
Solomon's kingdom in her presence:

*She said to the king, "The report I heard in my own
country about your achievements and your wisdom is
true. But I did not believe these things until I came and
saw with my own eyes. Indeed, not even half was told
me; in wisdom and wealth you have far exceeded the
report I heard. How happy your people must be! How
happy your officials, who continually stand before you
and hear your wisdom! Praise be to the Lord your God,
who has delighted in you and placed you on the throne
of Israel. Because of the Lord's eternal love for Israel, he
has made you king to maintain justice and righteousness
(1 Kings 10:6-9).*

Remarkable! Solomon must have been the envy of his
contemporaries. And yet, how come a man of his calibre who
had it all, now looks at life and death squarely in the face and
ask:

*What does man gain by all the toil at which he toils
under the sun? A generation goes, and a generation
comes... The sun rises, and the sun goes down... All
things are full of weariness; a man cannot utter it; the
eye is not satisfied with seeing, nor the ear filled with
hearing. What has been is what will be, and what has*

been done is what will be done, and there is nothing
new under the sun. Is there a thing of which it is said,
'See, this is new? (Ecclesiastes 1:3-5,8-10).

Honestly, I've come to like Solomon's realistic outlook of life. At least, he equips us to deal with life as it really is. Wishful thinking often does a lot of damage. To this end, Solomon gives a different perspective of life, contrary to the picture most people are privy to. For most people, we believe life would be much easier, fulfilling, and fun if we possessed all the things Solomon enjoyed. Consequently, a lot of people are struggling and toiling, all in the name of becoming successful in life and don't even care about the means to get there. Now, with Solomon's outlook of life, you can clearly deduce that all those things are simply not enough to have a successful, fulfilling, and peaceful life.

Solomon makes us understand that all those things are fleeting; they will one day pass away. This point is couched, as follows: *"I have seen all the things that are done under the sun; all of them are meaningless, a chasing after the wind"* (Ecclesiastes 1: 14). In actual fact, Solomon excels at getting us to think right because he attempts to redefine the meaning of life to mankind. Nevertheless, in spite of all the negative pictures he paints about life, he makes one splendid statement that gives a glimpse of hope that life is indeed profitable.

Consider this statement: *"The end of the matter; all has been heard. Fear God and keep his commandments, for this is the whole duty of man. For God will bring every deed into judgment, with every secret thing, whether good or evil"* (Ecclesiastes 12: 13,14).

Solomon opens our eyes of understanding to yet a very essential weapon for mastering the affairs of life- *the fear of God*. This theme will be explored in the next Chapter of this book. Does that mean that the fear of God is more important than wisdom? If so, could that mean that the popular saying that wisdom is all you need to have a prudent and fulfilling life-enough?

CHAPTER SIX

THE FEAR OF GOD IS KEY

•

The book of Ecclesiastes has a pastoral tone, motive, and message; partly because of the word-to *assemble* (O'Donnell, 2014, p.6). Serving God in obedience and honouring Him with a reverential fear for His deity is much simpler when you so badly need a breakthrough in order for you to move to your next level in life. People are mostly willing to humble and submit to the Lord in times of want than when they're in abundance. Yet, it should be much easier to claim your love for God in times of adversity and nothingness.

One sad and most common downfall of Christians, a pattern that is repeated many times over is when we begin to lose focus of where we've come from and how far the Lord has brought us. The tendency is to lose the reverential fear of God to live life as you please, especially, when you have been placed on a pedestal by the Lord. But God speaks to us through the prophet Moses to fear Him all the time for our own good.

*"And the L*ORD *commanded us to observe all these statutes, to fear the L*ORD *our God, for our good always, that He might preserve us alive, as it is this day. (Deuteronomy 6:24).*

This reverence of God helps us to take Him and His beneficial laws seriously. Being in harmony with the spiritual laws that govern the universe has astounding benefits. Many of these come in this life, but the greatest benefits will be experienced in the life to come. *"For bodily exercise profits a little, but godliness is profitable for all things, having promise of the life that now is and of that which is to come." (1 Timothy 4:8).*

David, the man who feared God

The ability to love the Lord and thank Him for His faithfulness; as well as, remembering how far He has brought you in life is one thing David never took for granted. Indeed, David was always mindful of his past and praised the Lord for his current circumstances. No wonder the Lord referred to him as "*the man after His own heart*".

Read what the Lord told the Prophet Samuel concerning David, after Saul, the king of Israel disobeyed the instructions of the Lord and was rejected: *But now your kingdom shall not continue. The Lord has sought for Himself a man after His own heart, and the Lord has commanded him to be commander over His people, because you have not kept what the Lord commanded you."* (1 Samuel 13:14).

This Biblical account has been corroborated in the book of Acts, where the Apostle Paul also speaks of God's impressions about King David; after the removal of Saul. God in His wisdom made David the king of Israel and testified concerning him, as follows: *"After removing Saul, he made David their king. He testified concerning him: 'I have found David son of Jesse a man after my own heart; he will do everything I want him to do"* (Acts 13:22).

We learn much of David's character and fear of God in the book of Psalms as he opened up his life for all to examine. David's life portrayed defeat and triumph. From all indications and per Biblical record, David's life depicted that he was far from being a perfect man. Moreover, David had his shortcomings as a man such that he committed a lot of terrible sins, including adultery, and ultimately murder.

An obvious question to address is: *Why and how could God still refer to such a man as a person after His own heart? What set David apart from the rest of the people in his generation?*

The answers to these questions will be *triple-fold*, as follows: (1) David feared the Lord, (2) David demonstrated his faith in the Lord, and (3) David exhibited gratefulness to the Lord. Christians should emulate these spiritual qualities and virtues to please God.

First, *David feared the Lord,* and had a deep desire to follow His will; as well as, do everything the Lord commanded him to do because his heart was pointed toward the Lord. Additionally, one amazing characteristic of David was how he never hesitated to make things right with God anytime he sinned against Him. All-in all, David held the Lord in high esteem.

Second, *David demonstrated his faith in the Lord.* Yes, David's faith was tested on a grand scale and he failed at times; yet, his imperfections, failures, and sins did not in any way prevent him from seeking the face of the God. Anytime David realized that he had sinned against the Lord, he sought to receive the Lord's forgiveness. For example, after he had committed adultery with Bathsheba (Uriah's wife and killed Uriah) and the Lord sent the Prophet Nathan to go and convict him of his sins (as recorded in 2 Samuel 11:2-5). As soon as, David was made aware of his sins, he became truly repentant and admitted his sins to Nathan. His response was: *"I have sinned against the Lord. Nathan replied, "The Lord has taken away your sin. You are not going to die."* (2 Samuel 12:13).

Admitting our sins and asking for forgiveness is only half of the equation. The other half is repentance, and David did that as well. The Bible records David's prayer of repentance in Psalm 51: *"Have mercy on me, O God, according to your steadfast love; according to your abundant mercy blot out my transgressions. Wash me thoroughly from my iniquity and cleanse me from my sin!"* (Psalm 51:1,2).

Three, *David was such a grateful person*. To a greater extent, just like Solomon, David's life was marked by seasons of prosperity, prestige, fame, among others, but through it all, he never forgot to thank the Lord for everything that he had. It is truly one of David's finest characteristics. Reflect on this passage of scripture:

> *Then King David went in and sat before the Lord; and he said: "Who am I, O Lord God? And what is my house, that You have brought me this far? And yet this was a small thing in Your sight, O Lord God; and You have also spoken of Your servant's house for a great while*

to come. Is this the manner of man, O Lord God? Now what more can David say to You? For You, Lord God, know Your servant. For Your word's sake, and according to Your own heart, you have done all these great things, to make Your servant know them. Therefore, you are great, O Lord God. For there is none like You, nor is there any God besides You, according to all that we have heard with our ears. And who is like Your people, like Israel, the one nation on the earth whom God went to redeem for Himself as a people, to make for Himself a name and to do for Yourself great and awesome deeds for Your land before Your people whom You redeemed for Yourself from Egypt, the nations, and their gods? For You have made Your people Israel Your very own people forever; and You, Lord, have become their God (2 Samuel 7:18-24).

Likewise, while on his death bed, read the advice he gave Solomon: *"Be kind to the sons of Barzillai from Gilead. Let them eat at your table. They helped me when I was fleeing from your brother Absalom"* (1 Kings 2:7). Wow, David is such a model to all Christians. He had such a gratitude heart for all mankind to emulate.

Serving the Lord and pursuing the will of God for his life was his utmost priority. And with the same mindset and humility of heart, he had left Christendom with that greatest legacy and for his son, Solomon to follow. When David was about to die, he instructed his son Solomon:

I'm about to leave this world. Be strong and mature. Fulfil your duty to the Lord your God. Obey his directions, laws, commands, rules, and written

instructions as they are recorded in Moses' Teachings.
Then you'll succeed in everything you do wherever you
may go. You'll succeed because the Lord will keep the
promise, he made to me: 'If your descendants are faithful
to me with all their hearts and lives, you will never fail
to have an heir on the throne of Israel (1 Kings 2:1-4).

Avoid Solomon's mistakes

Sadly enough, on the contrary Solomon did not do what his
father told him regarding the fear and honour of the Lord, as
explained in the preceding chapters. The comparison between
David and Solomon is provided in this scripture:

But King Solomon loved many foreign women, as well
as the daughter of Pharaoh: women of the Moabites,
Ammonites, Edomites, Sidonians, and Hittites from the
nations of whom the Lord had said to the children of
Israel, "You shall not intermarry with them, nor they
with you. Surely they will turn away your hearts after
their gods." Solomon clung to these in love. And he had
seven hundred wives, princesses, and three hundred
concubines; and his wives turned away his heart. For
it was so, when Solomon was old, that his wives turned
his heart after other gods; and his heart was not loyal to
the Lord his God, as was the heart of his father David.
For Solomon went after Ashtoreth the goddess of the
Sidonians, and after Milcom the abomination of the
Ammonites. Solomon did evil in the sight of the Lord,
and did not fully follow the Lord, as did his father
David. Then Solomon built a high place for Chemosh
the abomination of Moab, on the hill that is east of

Jerusalem, and for Molech the abomination of the people of Ammon. And he did likewise for all his foreign wives, who burned incense and sacrificed to their gods (1 Kings 11:1-8).

Anytime, I read the story of Solomon and consider all the opportunities the Lord brought his way; especially, after the Lord had endowed him with so much wisdom, I marvel at how such a wise and wealthy person ended life so poorly with lots of regrets and guilt. *How could such a wise person* who awed the Queen of Sheba with his great insight and the people in his kingdom with remarkable, astute counsel and ruling *not perceive that turning his heart away from the Lord was foolishness?*

This tells us that wisdom, prosperity, fame, and all the pleasures of the world cannot guarantee us the peace and fulfilment we seek in life. *Only the fear of God is the prerequisite for a life of peace and fulfilment.* This is the only thing that can guarantee us access into God's consistent blessings and true accomplishment in life. Solomon's attempted definition of the meaning of life in the book of Ecclesiastes concludes with the secret, which he let go during his heydays and ultimately cost him dearly.

After creating the awareness that all the pleasures of the world that man is fighting, struggling, killing, and doing all sorts of things for, were not enough to truly define life's true meaning, he concluded: *"Now all has been heard; here is the conclusion of the matter: Fear God and keep his commandments, for this is the duty of all mankind. For God will bring every deed into judgment, including every hidden thing, whether it is good or evil"* (Ecclesiastes 12:13,14).

No wonder in Proverbs 9:10 he emphasized: *"The fear of the LORD is the beginning of wisdom, and knowledge of the Holy One is understanding"* (Proverbs 9:10). This presupposes that without the fear of God the wisdom of man is foolishness. This is expressly stated by Solomon in the book of Proverbs, as follows; *"The fear of the LORD is the beginning of knowledge, but fools despise wisdom and instruction"* (Proverbs 1:7).

Solomon misused the opportunities God brought his way by serving other gods instead of the One who put him on the throne. Unlike his father-David, who appreciated the Lord for every single opportunity He brought his way; Solomon soon forgot all about the Lord and allowed the pleasures of the world to control his life. While David feared the Lord and therefore, was equally one of the wisest king's ever lived; Solomon's mistakes and sins caused him to end poorly. Nevertheless, Solomon wasn't selfish in telling us the secret to the true meaning of life, and the nugget of truth that could give us endless streams of victories as well as fulfilment in life-*the fear of God.*

What is the fear of God?

Dear reader this insight from Solomon should inform our Christian living on earth. Fearing the Lord does not mean we should be scared of being struck dead at any moment; even though, the Lord is the giver of life and He can decide to take one's life away as He pleases (Hebrews 9:27); but fearing God means- *making God a priority above all else that goes on in life.*

The Hebrew verb *yare* can mean "to fear, to respect, to reverence" and the Hebrew noun *yirah* "usually refers to the fear of God and is viewed as a positive quality. This fear acknowledges God's good intentions (Exodus 20:20). … This fear is produced by God's Word (Psalm 119:38; Proverbs 2:5) and makes a person receptive to wisdom and knowledge (Proverbs 1:7; 9:10)" (Warren Baker and Eugene Carpenter, *The Complete Word Study Dictionary: Old Testament*, 2003, pp. 470-471).

However, for the unbeliever, the fear of God is *the fear of the judgment of God and eternal death*, which is eternal separation from God (Luke 12:5; Hebrews 10:31).

To the believer, the fear of God is something much different because we have accepted His Lordship over our lives and are saved. Consequently, the believer's *fear of God is a deep reverence for God*. In the Book of Hebrews, Chapter 12 gives a good description of this: *"Therefore, since we are receiving a kingdom that cannot be shaken, let us be thankful, and so worship God acceptably with reverence and awe, for our 'God is a consuming fire"* (Hebrews 12:28, 29).

The reverence and awe are exactly what the fear of God means for the Christian and the motivating factor for us to surrender everything, wholly to the Creator of the Universe. Exactly what Solomon lacked after he acquired so much from the Lord because he didn't consider that the Lord gave him everything he had and so he should live a life that was pleasing to Him. For this reason, when you live life as you please, regardless of whether the Lord is pleased with you or not, it means you're living *a life of foolishness* like Solomon, which will lead to destruction, pain, shame, and regret. May the Lord forbid!

To the Christians, life means trusting the Lord and having absolute confidence in Him and willing to make sacrifices for Him. Sometimes, the sacrifices may cause you pain for a moment but in the end, you'll realize that He was actually using those pains for your own good (Romans 8:28). To fear the Lord means, *you take up your cross and follow Him, even when you don't know or can't fully comprehend where He's leading you to.*

Fearing God – Abraham's way

Abraham is another great example of a man who feared the Lord. He trusted in the Lord so much that he left the land of his birth where he was comfortable and familiar; to follow the Lord to a place he knew nothing about (Genesis 12). He was the man the Lord promised to make a *father of many nations* when he and his wife were still childless. When it seemed as though the promise was not coming to pass, he didn't lose hope but had confidence in the Lord. Furthermore, he knew that the Lord who had promised him was faithful and just to also bring the promise to pass (Hebrews 10:23).

Read this account from the record in the book of Romans:

Against all hope, Abraham in hope believed and so became the father of many nations, just as it had been said to him "So shall your offspring be." Without weakening in his faith, he faced the fact that his body was as good as dead since he was about a hundred years old and that Sarah's womb was also dead. Yet he did not waver through unbelief regarding the promise of God,

but was strengthened in his faith and gave glory to God,
being fully persuaded that God had power to do what
he had promised. This is why "it was credited to him as
righteousness (Romans 4:18-22).

Abraham waited 25 years before this promise came to pass (Genesis 17). Not only did he trust the Lord to give him a son in his old age, he also trusted the Lord to bring Isaac back to life and was willing to offer him; the child of promise as a sacrifice to the Lord when the Lord requested him to do just that. Reflect on this passage:

Sometime later God tested Abraham. He said to him,
"Abraham!" "Here I am," he replied. Then God said,
"Take your son, your only son, whom you love Isaac and
go to the region of Moriah. Sacrifice him there as a burnt
offering on a mountain I will show you "Early the next
morning Abraham got up and loaded his donkey. He took
with him two of his servants and his son Isaac. When he
had cut enough wood for the burnt offering, he set out
for the place God had told him about. On the third day
Abraham looked up and saw the place in the distance.
He said to his servants, "Stay here with the donkey while
I and the boy go over there. We will worship and then we
will come back to you (Genesis 22:1-5).

Abraham exhibited this trust solely in the sovereign Lord. You see, often we're tempted to brush through Abraham's story and see him as some super human who showed no emotions about going to sacrifice *the son*. I believe the decision wasn't an easy one for Abraham at all. Perhaps, he wept, became confused, and sad at the thought of not seeing his son again.

However, the fear of God and his trust in Him overcame every emotion and misgiving he had regarding what the Lord had requested from him. At the end of the story, God testified about Abraham saying, *".... now I know you fear God, ..."* (Genesis 22:12).

You cannot claim you fear God when you're not willing to fully obey everything He tells you to do. Typically, God-fearing people make good citizens because: (i) they are always obedient to the higher laws of God; then, (ii) to the laws of the land. Even though, this might not make them happy in life; yet it will make others happy and ultimately glorify God. When you fear God, you're willing to love and value His presence above all.

David loved the presence of God so much that he says in Psalm 16: *"in your presence there is fullness of joy"* (Psalm 16:11). When you fear the Lord, you're always eager to have fellowship with Him and wait on Him for instructions before you proceed to take decisions. As a result, out of reverence for the Lord, we choose to love what He loves and hate what He hates. Solomon lacked this virtue and ended up living a life of regret and pain.

Some benefits of the fear of the Lord

Looking at the examples of David and Abraham in their fear of God as discussed above, I can say that, the fear of God helps us have a proper, humble perspective of ourselves in relation to our awesome God; it helps us in times of trials and temptation when we need to remember the serious consequences of disobeying God; and it motivates us to become more like our loving Creator. This will surely bring eternal benefits: It will become a fountain of life by turning you away from the snare of death, guarantees your hope, and brings you satisfaction and God's deliverance.

♦ *"The fear of the LORD is a fountain of life, to turn one away from the snares of death" (Proverbs 14:27).*

♦ *"Do not let your heart envy sinners, but be zealous for the fear of the LORD all the day; for surely there is a hereafter, and your hope will not be cut off" (Proverbs 23:17-18).*

♦ *"The fear of the LORD leads to life, and he who has it will abide in satisfaction; he will not be visited with evil" (Proverbs 19:23).*

♦ *"Behold, the eye of the LORD is on those who fear Him, On those who hope for His loving-kindness, To deliver their soul from death And to keep them alive in famine" (Psalm 33:18-19)*

The fear of God is key for proper functioning in wisdom. The wisdom will lead you into making the right choices and decisions. Solomon scripts it down for all mankind to understand that, the fear of the Lord is essential for one's life to have true meaning and essence. There is the urgent need to give up attempts to comprehend God and His actions and to advocate the need to lead a life of hospitality and generosity, table fellowship, and meaningful labor; as well as the good life, which is pleasing to God (Levicheva, 2014). *What is your choice?* The fear of the Lord or the pleasures of the world?

CHAPTER SEVEN

FIGURING IT OUT

•

The book of Ecclesiastes has identified the critical problems of the human conditions as determined by modern men but offers in several ways a feasible and reasonable attitude towards contemporary life (Marcus, 2000). It is not at all satisfying to think your life has no meaning than just being born, living a short while, then dying. That's so wrong; yet there is nothing in the Bible that says what the meaning of life is, but the Bible suggests God's purposes for us to accomplish to find meaning and fulfilment in our lives.

There is a reason God created you on this earth. Your life has meaning because He had a specific thing in mind when He created you, and until you *figure out* that specific reason, life would only be like an experiment without a clear direction or future. When you search Scriptures, you'll identify many men and women who identified the reason for their existence and allowed the Lord to use them to accomplish that purpose. For example, The Lord said concerning Jeremiah: *"Before I formed*

you in the womb I knew you, before you were born I set you apart;
I appointed you as a prophet to the nations" (Jeremiah 1:5).

Solomon would have been right when he said everything is meaningless. Yet, this isn't God's true intent for His children. The difference between those who are successful and living fulfilled lives and those who are not is as a result of one thing- *the former has found the meaning of their lives by figuring out what they were born to do, and allowed the Lord to bring that meaning into fruition.*

God's will for your life is not for you to die empty; leaving this world happy and fulfilled as Jesus did on the cross and said *"It is finished"* (John 19:30) and as Apostle Paul said *"I have fought the good fight, I have run the race, I have kept the faith"* (2 Timothy 4:7). In the case of Abraham, he died at a good old age, having lived a long and satisfying life (Genesis 25:8). On his part, David died after serving God's purpose in his generation (Acts 13:36). Paul came to the end of his life with no regrets of how he had lived and was very confident of the future (2 Timothy 4:6-8).

There are *three* widespread means by which people deal with the meaninglessness of which Solomon writes: (I) **escapism**, some people deal with bleak realities through watching games, playing with kids, going to work, taking family vacation, loving the wife; and watching the game, watching the game, watching the game; (II) **nihilism**, others are more philosophical about life; and (III) **hedonism**, most people are not honest enough and so live for pleasure as the ultimate pursuit (O'Donnell, 2014, pp.23-26).

70

The Basic Questions All Must Answer

In figuring out God's purpose for your life, there are five basic questions to seek answers to address, as follows: *(a) who am I? (b) Where am I from? (c) Why am I here? (d) What can I do? and (e) where am I going?*

1. **Who Am I?** *This is a question of identity.*

If you don't establish your true identity you may live life anyhow you please. Without a full understanding of the price Christ has paid on the cross for you, you may waste your life away like Solomon did. It is important you find out who you really are and that can only be found in the Word of God. What has God said concerning the Christian? That's where your true identity emanates from not your past or what others say about you. God is your creator and He alone can tell you what your identity is. Your identity is wrapped up in the Word of God. Start searching the Word: *"But you are a chosen people, a royal priesthood, a holy nation, God's special possession, that you may declare the praises of him who called you out of darkness into his wonderful light. Once you were not a people, but now you are the people of God; once you had not received mercy, but now you have received mercy"* (1 Peter 2:9).

2. **Where Am I from**? – *This has got to do with your heritage.*

After identifying who you are based on what the Word of God tells you; then, you can clearly find out where you're from. This will help you know where you're going next and which choices and decisions to make. It is vital to note that

71

this heritage does not refer to your ethnic background, but rather, the ideal source where you're from.

We are created by God and have our being in Him. Paul pointed to this when he addressed the Athenians in Acts 17:

> *For all the Athenians and the foreigners who were there spent their time in nothing else but either to tell or to hear some new thing. Then Paul stood in the midst of the Areopagus and said, "Men of Athens, I perceive that in all things you are very religious; for as I was passing through and considering the objects of your worship, I even found an altar with this inscription: … Therefore, the One whom you worship without knowing, Him I proclaim to you: God, who made the world and everything in it, since He is Lord of heaven and earth, does not dwell in temples made with hands. Nor is He worshiped with men's hands, as though He needed anything, since He gives to all life, breath, and all things. And He has made from one blood every nation of men to dwell on all the face of the earth, and has determined their pre-appointed times and the boundaries of their dwellings, so that they should seek the Lord, in the hope that they might grope for Him and find Him, though He is not far from each one of us; for in Him we live and move and have our being, as also some of your own poets have said, 'For we are also His offspring (Acts 17:21-28).*

When you have an understanding of your heritage, it will change your perspective on life. It will also help you know where you're going and the best decisions to make to get there.

In the case of Abraham, he was a man who understood who he was and where he came from. This in no doubt, gave him a sense of direction in life. His whole life was not meaningless despite the many challenges and difficulties that he went through, neither did he glory in the material blessings that God gifted him. The Bible records:

> By faith Abraham obeyed when he was called to go out to the place which he would receive as an inheritance. And he went out, not knowing where he was going. By faith he dwelt in the land of promise as in a foreign country, dwelling in tents with Isaac and Jacob, the heirs with him of the same promise; for he waited for the city which has foundations, whose builder and maker is God (Hebrews 11:8-10).

In Galatians 3, the Bible says: *"If you belong to Christ, then you are Abraham's seed, and heirs according to the promise"* (Galatians 3:29). Similarly, in showing Christians our heritage and how it affects how we view life and helps in making the right choices, the Bible says concerning our forefathers in the faith:

> All these people were still living by faith when they died. They did not receive the things promised; they only saw them and welcomed them from a distance, admitting that they were foreigners and strangers on earth. People who say such things show that they are looking for a country of their own. If they had been thinking of the country they had left, they would have had opportunity to return. Instead, they were longing for a better country a heavenly one. Therefore, God is not ashamed to be

called their God, for he has prepared a city for them (Hebrews 11:13-16).

3. **Why Am I Here?** – *This is a question of purpose.*

The Lord in Jeremiah 29 said: *"For I know the plans I have for you," declares the Lord, "plans to prosper you and not to harm you, plans to give you hope and a future"* (Jeremiah 29:11). The Lord alone knows His plans for you and what He's called you to do. You need to find out from Him what these plans are and live accordingly. But do not forget, that, we are all stewards of God's gracious gifts to us; this is applicable to all.

4. **What Can I Do?** – *This is associated with your gifts, abilities, or potentials*

Until you discover your potentials, you cannot make the most of it. God has deposited a gift in you which when identified and harnessed can help you impact your world positively. Use your life, your talent, your gift, and whatever you have to glorify God by serving others. Peter says in his first epistle Chapter 4:

> *But the end of all things is at hand; therefore be serious and watchful in your prayers. And above all things have fervent love for one another, for "love will cover a multitude of sins." Be hospitable to one another without grumbling. As each one has received a gift, minister it to one another, as good stewards of the manifold grace of God. If anyone speaks, let him speak as the oracles of God. If anyone ministers, let him do it as with the ability which God supplies, that in all things God may*

be glorified through Jesus Christ, to whom belong the glory and the dominion forever and ever. Amen (1 Peter 4:7-11).

Don't hold back anymore, let the world benefit from the gift God has given to you. This is what will give your life a meaning.

5. **Where Am I Going?** – *This is about your destiny.*

If you don't know where you're going, you may mistake a '*rest stop*' to mean '*bus stop*'. Thus, a clear sense of the level God wants to take you to, you may become complacent with your little achievements and may in the end turn your heart from the Lord like Solomon did. *"It's not over, until the Lord says it's over"*-T.D. JAKES (Retrieved from https://www.pinterest.com/pin/551761391822320223/-accessed on 08/17/2019). God's utmost desire is for you to discover your purpose for life (Proverbs 19:21).

The majority of frustrated Christians who complain about the fact that life has no meaning haven't been able to address the five questions discussed above. *"The greatest tragedy in life is not death, the greatest tragedy in life is a life without a purpose. A dead man is no longer accountable to why he's breathing but you who are living must give account"*-Myles Munroe (Retrieved from http://infoblique.blogspot.com/2016/08/discovering-god-purpose-for-your-life.html-accessed on 08/17/2019). When you figure out who God has made you to be, and latch on to what He says about you and reject the worrywarts you don't toil in life. This is because you will become focused on pursuing your purpose and giving your life meaning. As a result, you're protected from needlessly expending your energy in areas outside God's will for your life.

Hasrat (2019) examined gender and age differences in the sources of meaning in life and concluded that age and gender has a significant interaction effect on *achievement* (*fair treatment* and *intimacy*); because both determinants increased with age. Consequently, *achievement* as a source of meaning has a significant relationship with gender where males scored higher than females (Hasrat, 2019). Therefore, wealth, prestige among others, will surely come your way when you pursue the purpose of God for your life.

This is where you need to be careful not to turn your heart away from the Lord like Solomon did, and misuse the resources God brings your way. Everything God blesses you with is to help promote and expand His kingdom and also to help others climb the success ladder. Until you find why God made you, you'll never have meaning in life. *Have you figured it out?*

CHAPTER EIGHT

THERE IS NOTHING NEW UNDER THE SUN

•

King Solomon saw plenty of motions on the earth's surface and tried several means of making life meaningful as we have seen in the previous chapters of this book; through the building of magnificent palace, forming alliances with heathen kings, marrying different women, applying himself to knowledge and wisdom, and many more; yet there was no promotion of a truly profitable life for him. *What is the reason?* The possible answer is that he left God out of his pursuits.

One key phrase of his writing is: "*under the sun*" (verse 9). This phrase "*under the sun*" is equivalent to drawing a horizontal line between earthly and heavenly realities but focusing entirely or almost entirely on the earthly ones. If a person does this; then, we must accept the fruit, as described by Solomon to be inevitably vanity because that is all that carnality can produce. Nevertheless, there is a higher reality in existence, and that is what Solomon urges us to relate to. The nature of

God in Christ is the spiritual reality we have been created to participate in. This has been described in the Bible as: *"That which has been is what will be, that which is done is what will be done, and there is nothing new under the sun"* (Ecclesiastes 1:9).

There is nothing new under the sun. I pose the question: *Is this statement true?* What about the inventions we see around the world? If we look back to the *1900s* and compare those times with the world today, we see many changes that have occurred; and for that reason, makes it difficult to grasp what Solomon is saying about life-*"there is nothing new under the sun"* Back then, there were no radios, televisions, computers, the internet, and the smart phones. Likewise, there were no or limited expressways, mass production of cars, airplanes, birth control pill, magnetic resonance imaging machines to produce detailed pictures of parts of the human body; as well as, no atomic bomb, understanding of *deoxyribonucleic acid* or DNA, or gene splicing.

Today, we have all these things which probably never existed before. Now we live in the information age and can attest to the impact of technological advancements on human life. Some futurists have propounded the establishment of colonies on the planet Mars. Others have argued that very soon telephones will be fitted into a piece of jewellery. Similarly, a few have portended that man will be swallowing micro robots that will perform surgeries on humans' internal organs. Additionally, predictions about various gizmos and gadgets have surfaced; however, a more basic prediction of the overall trend is involved with machines becoming more like human and humans becoming more like machines.

In the *1900s*, no one anticipated the impact of the following persons: Einstein, Lenin, Churchill, Hitler, Gandhi, Hugh Hefner, Martin Luther King, Nelson Mandela, Osama bin Laden, and many more. Yet, people could change the course of history in ways that none of us could predict with any degree of accuracy. Indeed, per Solomon *"there is nothing new under the sun"* Solomon touched on the basic principles of life and not the methods, which I believe; will be understood by the time you finish reading this chapter.

Man is perceived to be chasing after a mirage such that the faster we run, the farther away our dreams move from us. As a result, life without God is like the cycles of nature because there are plenty of motions but no advancement. Consequently, life appears to be a depressing picture of tedious meaninglessness. King Solomon captured this as follows:

> *All things are full of labor; man cannot express it. The eye is not satisfied with seeing, nor the ear filled with hearing. That which has been is what will be, that which is done is what will be done, and there is nothing new under the sun. Is there anything of which it may be said, "See this is new?" It has already been in ancient times before us (Ecclesiastes 1:8-10).*

The earth is characterized by a great deal of activity but it is essentially purposeless with a great deal of sound and fury; with no advancement in the quality of life, and devoid of a purposeful direction or perspective from God. However, it is only in Him that we find the true meaning of life. We are by no means suggesting that mankind is moving about and not making any advancement that improves the way life is lived on earth. Like Solomon as with many people, during the latter part of his life left God out of his life but until God is found; all human inventions or innovations cannot bring mankind to the desired place where his creator wants him to be. God is the answer but unfortunately, many have left Him out of their lives and only going after new inventions.

In the book of Acts, we are informed in chapter 17, that the Epicurean and stoic philosophers spent all their time in nothing else, except to tell and listen to new things, as follows:

> *Then certain Epicurean and Stoic philosophers encountered him. And some said, "What does this babbler want to say?" Others said, "He seems to be a proclaimer of foreign gods," because he preached to them Jesus and the resurrection. And they took him and brought him to the Areopagus, saying, "May we know what this new doctrine is of which you speak? For you are bringing some strange things to our ears. Therefore, we want to know what these things mean." For all the Athenians and the foreigners who were there spent their time in nothing else but either to tell or to hear some new thing (Acts 17:16-21).*

While the *Epicureans* were followers of a philosopher named Epicurus, who taught that pleasure and not the pursuit of knowledge is the chief end of life; the *Stoic* on the other hand, were pantheists, who believed in wisdom and being free from intense emotion, unmoved by joy or grief, willingly submissive to natural law. To them, man is at the center of all things. An apt question to ask is: *Was this not the same approach Solomon utilized to find the meaning of life?* Keep in mind that before

Solomon was made king of Israel, God had given laws that should govern kings in the book of Deuteronomy, as follows:

> *When you come to the land which the Lord your God is giving you, and possess it and dwell in it, and say, 'I will set a king over me like all the nations that are around me,' you shall surely set a king over you whom the Lord your God chooses; one from among your brethren you shall set as king over you; you may not set a foreigner over you, who is not your brother. But he shall not multiply horses for himself, nor cause the people to return to Egypt to multiply horses, for the Lord has said to you, 'You shall not return that way again.' Neither shall he multiply wives for himself, lest his heart turn away; nor shall he greatly multiply silver and gold for himself. "Also, it shall be, when he sits on the throne of his kingdom, that he shall write for himself a copy of this law in a book, from the one before the priests, the Levites. And it shall be with him, and he shall read it all the days of his life, that he may learn to fear the Lord his God and be careful to observe all the words of this law and these statutes, that his heart may not be lifted above his brethren, that he may not turn aside from the commandment to the right hand or to the left, and that he may prolong his days in his kingdom, he and his children in the midst of Israel (Deuteronomy 17:14-20).*

The above scripture is the principles God gave to govern kings of Israel. So, for Solomon, there was a clear divine path set for him to follow, as summed up below-the king: (1) must be a man of God's choice, (2) must not depend on natural means for victory, (3) must not lead people back to slavery, (4) must not indulge in lustful and worldly pleasure, (5) must eschew greed, and (6) must not be proud. Instead, (7) must delight in the law of God. Yet, *what do we see in Solomon's life at the end?* He violated almost every one of these principal orders to his own destruction and the ruin of his kingdom (1 Kings 10:14-29; 11:1-8). As a consequence:

> *So, the LORD became angry with Solomon, because his heart had turned from the LORD God of Israel, who had appeared to him twice, and had commanded him concerning this thing, that he should not go after other gods; but he did not keep what the LORD had commanded (1Kings 11:9-10).*

Do not leave God out

Precious reader, leaving God out of life is the gravest mistake one can ever make because such a path only leads to idolatry. Sadly, this is exactly what Solomon did; he tried new things with a view to finding happiness but it became only a manifestation of humanity-ruined nature, which leads to vanity as was the case of the Epicurean and Stoic philosophers in Acts, as mentioned earlier. Consider the following passage of Scripture: *"Now while Paul waited for them at Athens, his spirit was provoked within him when he saw that the city was given over to idols"* (Acts 17:16). Paul had to present the gospel of Jesus Christ as the *only way* through which man could get back into a relationship with God, his creator and also find true meaning, purpose, and satisfaction in life.

The old *Adam* is in us all but until that is changed, nothing is new. In fact, we do not condemn new ideas and inventions but when it comes to finding true meaning and purpose in life, nothing new is offered. Even though, with advancement in civilization, there is a multiplication in the enjoyment of life, as well as, a refinement of pleasure. However, this does not bring us nearer to complete satisfaction because they do not change who we are by nature – *sinners* and *enemies of God*. God originally gave man a sure means to have a meaningful life – *trusting and obeying* Him, but we have always neglected what God has given us for new things.

A vital element that is missing from life is the overall perspective we have regarding life itself, combined with the lack of a relationship with God. For example, the entertainment industry thrives on this desire to fill people's need for emotional satisfaction by devising new angles to the same old stories. However, what this need really exposes us to is that, our present life, when combined with what we are looking forward to in the future, is not fulfilling enough to satisfy us. Likewise, entrepreneurs take advantage of this need to have new, better, bigger, redesigned, more serviceable, more attractive, faster, safer, and more economical models each year just to make money. Hence, understanding this desire for new things apart from God is critical from this text: *"....... Also, He has put eternity in their hearts, except that no one can find out the work that God does from beginning to end"* (Ecclesiastes 3:11).

God created man as a religious being, who should live in close relationship with God the creator in obedience to Him; however, mankind sought for new ways of improving upon life and that led to the fall; despite this knowledge, this is the course or path mankind has been treading after the fall. Most people live by the same basic pattern by which Adam and Eve followed after God kicked them out of the Garden; such as trying to improve the quality of life, searching for better ways of life, revolving around those that will fill us with joy and our minds with satisfaction; but always become disillusioned in all we do without God by trying new things, which fail to produce the expected result – satisfaction in life. This state of affairs is couched in the book of Ecclesiastes, as follows: *"All things are full of labor; Man cannot express it. The eye is not satisfied with seeing, Nor the ear filled with hearing"* (Ecclesiastes 1:8).

Only God Creates New Things

Only God can create new things, and he begins by making sinners *new creature* when we trust Jesus Christ to save us. The Bible states: *"Therefore, if anyone is in Christ, he is a new creation; old things have passed away; behold, all things have become new"* (2 Corinthians 5:17). Once God comes into our lives, He makes us anew and then we can walk *in newness of life*, because the old self who neglects God is buried in Christ so that the new man created in Christ will live here on earth. Consider this: *"Therefore, we were buried with Him through baptism into death, that just as Christ was raised from the dead by the glory of the Father, even so we also should walk in newness of life"* (Romans 6:4).

As believers we will enjoy a new heaven and a new earth that God is preparing for those who receive Jesus as Lord and savior. *"Now I saw a new heaven and a new earth, for the first heaven and the first earth had passed away. Also, there was no more sea"* (Revelations 21:1). By implication, what Solomon is saying is that things are wearisome. The question is: *Do you agree with Solomon's assessment to this point? Is he right in his litany of mankind's purposelessness, monotonous life that leads nowhere?* Solomon has achieved the purpose of making us appreciate that *vanity of vanities* is the only honest assessment of life on earth as long as people are persistently, but without a large measure of truth, seeking purpose and profit in life without God.

God is the source of all new things and so without Him, nothing is new. The major problem is that our work adds nothing new to this world because in Ecclesiastes 1:4-8, Solomon describes this repetitiveness and lack of originality of our human activities in relation to the earth's circularity as opposed to its stability (O'Donnell, 2014, pp.18-19). Additionally, our work will not be remembered because nothing new is remembered; as a result, *"there is no remembrance for former things, nor will there be any remembrance of later things yet to be among those who came after"* (Ecclesiastes 1:11- O'Donnell, 2014, p.21).

Let us consider some few examples: *first*, in Genesis 1, God created the heaven and the earth, and in the process of making it more functional and habitable, He created *light,* long before man through His enablement invented electricity. Likewise, *birds* were created by God to fly around before an airplane was invented. Similarly, there were *rivers* watering the Garden of Eden before man could ever think of irrigation methods and devices.

Second, in Genesis 6 and 7, Noah builds an *ark* according to God's command and specifications. This was done back in the ancient times (one would say primitive times), yet, somebody was able to construct an ocean liner that could wither the *tsunami* of the times. Additionally, in Genesis 11, we are informed of how man was able to *use bricks* instead of stone and tar for mortar, to build a city with a tower that was higher than most of the modern-day towers and skyscrapers. The book of Jubilees mentions the tower's height as being eight thousand one hundred fifty feet (8,150ft), or about 1.6 miles high. I argue that is higher than "*the Twin Towers*" which is believed to be about 1,368ft and 1,362ft respectively.

Three, in the book of Jonah, we are told in Chapter 1 and verse 17 of how God who created all things, made a dwelling for Jonah at the *belly of the sea.* Jonah was swallowed by a big fish that was prepared by God and Jonah lived there for three days. Surprisingly, the fish carried Jonah to Nineveh, the right place where God wanted him to be. The concept of submarine is birthed here. *Isn't it amazing?* More so, airplanes and rockets are not new ideas because before man invented them, God had demonstrated the principle of *rapturing* Elijah in 2 Kings 2. Likewise, the book of Ezra and 1Kings inform us of how people were enabled by the Spirit of God to build magnificent buildings with wooding floors and gold furnishings.

Four, fast forwarding to the New Testament, God miraculously saved Peter from prison in Acts 12, where the *prison doors* opened without any human intervention. Do you see the link between this miracle and the concept of auto doors? Now, from the examples cited above, it is obvious that God is the source of all creation and that, if man is able to create or invent something he may call new, I contend that it is only a discovery of what God the creator has covered, and as such inventions should become a revelation of the power of the provider – God who is the creator and from whom all things come into being: "*That which hath been is now, and that which is to be hath already been*" (Ecclesiastes 3:15).

Solomon realized that whatever we tend to call new inventions are only discoveries of what God has created and made possible; and so, subsequently, in his opening remarks, Solomon launches into a series of illustrations drawn from the earth's natural cycles and then applies them as evidence to support the kind of environment man's life is built upon:

> *One generation passes away, and another generation comes; but the earth abides forever. The sun also rises, and the sun goes down, and hastens to the place where it arose. The wind goes toward the south and turns around to the north; the wind whirls about continually and comes again on its circuit. All the rivers run into the sea, yet the sea is not full; to the place from which the rivers come, there they return again (Ecclesiastes 1:4-7).*

A new generation is born into the world every 20 to 25 years, creating the impression that something is actually happening, but nothing really is; except that the older generation is dying off. A seemingly endless procession of people come and go, but this was not how God created mankind to be. We were originally created religious beings to have immortality but the fall of Adam and Eve in the Garden of Eden and its effects on all human race has had grave alteration in life. So, *why do we sometimes think that things are new?* The answer is simple: we have bad memories and we don't read the minutes of the previous meeting. The book of Ecclesiastes states: *"There is no remembrance of former things, nor will there be any remembrance of things that are to come by those who will come after"* (Ecclesiastes 1:11).

Nothing changes man's relationship with God despite all inventions and other forms of technological advancements. The repetitiveness of activities largely occurs in nature's cycles, but human life remains generally unchanged and static, thus, going nowhere. The earth and its systems permanently function as God had designed them, but man is transient; a pilgrim living in a constant state of repeated change. What is needed is God; until then, no matter what we can do, the results will be the same – *vanity* because man is lost.

No human achievement can mend the broken relationship with God the creator and set right all the evils that exist in this world. Solomon's testimony that follows in Ecclesiastes 1:12-18, shows that, our self-efforts are not enough in finding purpose and meaning in life:

I, the Preacher, was king over Israel in Jerusalem. And I set my heart to seek and search out by wisdom concerning all that is done under heaven; this burdensome task God has given to the sons of man, by which they may be exercised. I have seen all the works that are done under the sun; and indeed, all is vanity and grasping for the wind. What is crooked cannot be made straight, and what is lacking cannot be numbered. I communed with my heart, saying, "Look, I have attained greatness, and have gained more wisdom than all who were before me in Jerusalem. My heart has understood great wisdom and knowledge" And I set my heart to know wisdom and to know madness and folly. I perceived that this also is grasping for the wind. For in much wisdom is much grief, and he who increases knowledge increases sorrow (Ecclesiastes 1:12-18).

Did you read the above passage? There is more trouble and sorrow in our present world despite the increase of wisdom, new ideas, philosophies, new discoveries; or if you want, creations and inventions. The underlining principle is *that: mankind has rejected God's authority over his life and therefore has lost the true meaning of life.* The increase of knowledge through the advancement of technology has reached a stage where there is the belief that man is his own God. There is no regard for God by people who call themselves *evolutionists*; however, this is not a new thing because in the book of Genesis, Adam and Eve rejected God and wanted to be wise. Man abandoned the divine path given him, but the result was a disaster.

Solomon was blessed by God and tried to use the wisdom, power, talent, and wealth God had given him to play God, but achieved nothing. Furthermore, looking at our today's world, I can infer that we are in dangerous times because we tend to act as though God does not matter; and as a result, we are masters of our own destiny. While God created humanity to rule certain aspects of creation; that does not make us *gods*, who are responsible to none but ourselves. Accordingly, in the book of Romans, Paul writes "*although they knew God, they did not glorify Him as God, nor were thankful, but became futile in their thoughts, and their foolish hearts were darkened. Professing to be wise, they became fools*" (Romans 1:21-22).

The things man can do can never be a substitute for finding meaningfulness in life, yet, man continued the same path. Man's need in this life is finding God; for without Him, all is meaningless. My question is: *Are you surprised?* No, do not be. What Solomon experienced in times of old is the same thing happening now. Mankind is evolving, or we are actually devolving: We started high (created in the image of God) and because of sin, sank lower than how we were originally created (man lost the glory of God). For this reason, Douglas S. O'Donnell (2014) offered this: *Jesus Christ redeemed us from the vanity that Pastor Solomon so wrestled with and suffered under by subjecting himself to our temporary, meaningless, futile, incomprehensible, incongruous, absurd, smoke-curling-up-into-the air, mere-breath, vain life. He was born under the sun. He toiled under the sun. He suffered under the sun. He died under the sun. But in his subjection to be the curse of death by his own death on the cross, the son of God redeemed us from the curse (Galatians 3:13). By his resurrection, he restored meaning to our toil. And by his return, he will exact every injustice and elucidate every absurdity as he ushers those who fear the Lord into the glorious presence of our all-wise, never-completely-comprehensible God (pp.12-13).*

All said and done it can be concluded that by the expression "There is nothing new under the sun" which is used 29 times only in Ecclesiastes (and nowhere else in Scripture), Solomon was emphasizing the cyclical nature of natural phenomena... the rising and setting of the sun, activities of seas, river courses, wind direction, and the natural orientation of human nature, activities , and pursuits. These things may take on a semblance of novelty but they are intrinsically the same. The veneer may be splashy and flashy but it remains quintessentially the same.

Furthermore when one considers the inventions and discoveries taking place in our world today, one may wonder whether Solomon was altogether right by saying there is nothing new under the sun, considering the creation of the internet, smart phones, supersonic jets, precision bombers, autonomous/driverless cars, spaceships and exploration, nuclear weapons, amazing aspects of artificial intelligence, discoveries and inventions in medical science, etc.

A careful examination of the etymology of the terms we use, "invention" and "discover" will settle the issue. In modern usage, to "invent" means to fabricate something new. The root of the Latin word "*invenire*" (in- come, into). The ordinary usage of "discover" implies coming upon something which had been or existed but unknown. The root of the Latin word is "*discooperire*" which also means "to make known by removing the cover". It is made up of two words, "dis" ("opposite of") and "*cooperire*" ("to cover"). The joint word simply means to "uncover/remove the cover").

Simply put, the roots of the two words mean the same, "to uncover/remove the cover". For example, when scientists discovered the latest planet "Kepler 69C in June 2018. It was just a discovery; they did not create or invent it. It had been there for ages past; they simply removed the cover for us. Similarly, although supersonic jets are not mentioned by name in the Bible, the laws of physics on which they were built had long existed. (We must understand that Biblical history is only a little part of world history. For example, before the construction of the Tower of Babel 2,100 years before Christ was born, Babylon and Egypt already existed as empires with their developed languages, academic institutions, engineers, civil servants. As early as 586 BCE, the Babylonians were already using bombs in warfare (Ezek. 21 and 26).

I pose the question: *What is new under the sun?*

CHAPTER NINE

CHRIST GIVES MEANING TO LIFE

•

Pargament and Hahn (1986) conducted a research on human efforts to seek meaning to life. These researchers posited that people turn to God for help in coping and more commonly as a source of support during stress than as a moral guide or as an antidote to an unjust world. The scripture points out clearly that "*The Word gave life to everything that was created, and his life brought light to everyone*" (John 1:4, Retrieved from https://www.haikudeck.com-accessed on 08/17/2019). More so, the findings suggest the need for further integration of religious concepts into the general attributions and coping literature (Pargament & Hahn, 1986, p.193). Additionally, Exline, Prince-Paul, Root, and Peereboom (2013) elaborated that (a) *prayer was the most highly endorsed strategy for managing conflicts with God*; other commonly endorsed strategies included: (b) reading sacred texts, (c) handling the feeling on one's own, and (d) conversations with friends, family, clergy, or hospice staff. However, self-help resources and therapy were less popular options (p.369).

If Christians and unbelievers all end up in the same place after death, then would there be a practical reason for each of us to act morally and in obedience to the Word of God? *Have you thought of this?* If after making it in life, you spend all the wealth you've accumulated on drugs to keep you healthy and alive, then will life truly have a meaning? Likewise, if there is no God; then, man and all of creation are hopeless just like a prisoner condemned to death and awaiting his or her unavoidable execution.

If there is no God, and there is no immortality, then life would be without value and meaning. Thus, if each individual passes out of existence when he dies, with no hope of eternity; *what ultimately can be the meaning of life? Would it even matter whether (s)he ever existed at all?* Life may be important relative to certain other events, but *what is the ultimate significance of any of those events*? If all the events are meaningless; or "*a chasing after the wind*", then, *what can be the ultimate meaning of influencing any of them?* Eventually, it makes no difference.

Additional questions to be posed encompass: (i) *Do you understand the magnitude of the alternatives before us?* This means that if God exists, then there is hope for man. But if God did not exist, then what we will be left with is despair. (ii) *Do you understand why the question of God's existence and the price Christ paid for man on the cross is so vital to man?* Maybe you've heard about the man whose goal in life was to climb a certain mountain. When he finally reached the top of the mountain, he was terribly disappointed because there was nowhere else for him to go, and something was still missing in his life. Just like Solomon who had all the pleasures of the world at his disposal; and yet, wasn't satisfied with life because at the peak of his life, he realized there was something missing in his life.

Will Your Anchor Hold?

The biblical story of the rich man and Lazarus in the New Testament is a good lesson on this. Let us consider Jesus' teaching on life in this passage:

> *There was a rich man who was dressed in purple and fine linen and lived in luxury every day. At his gate was laid a beggar named Lazarus, covered with sores and longing to eat what fell from the rich man's table. Even the dogs came and licked his sores. "The time came when the beggar died and the angels carried him to Abraham's side. The rich man also died and was buried. In Hades, where he was in torment, he looked up and saw Abraham far away, with Lazarus by his side. So, he called to him, 'Father Abraham, have pity on me and send Lazarus to dip the tip of his finger in water and cool my tongue, because I am in agony in this fire.' "But Abraham replied, 'Son, remember that in your lifetime you received your good things, while Lazarus received bad things, but now he is comforted here and you are in agony. And besides all this, between us and you a great chasm has been set in place, so that those who want to go from here to you cannot, nor can anyone cross over from there to us.' "He answered, 'Then I beg you, father, send Lazarus to my family, for I have five brothers. Let him warn them, so that they will not also come to this*

place of torment.' "Abraham replied, 'They have Moses and the Prophets; let them listen to them.' "'No, father Abraham,' he said, 'but if someone from the dead goes to them, they will repent.' "He said to him, 'If they do not listen to Moses and the Prophets, they will not be convinced even if someone rises from the dead (Luke 16:19-31).

Here, Jesus was illustrating the situation of the Pharisees who loved money and those who spend all their time idolizing wealth (verse 14). He uses a rich man and Lazarus to reveal that life here on earth, if it be without Christ, is all but vanity no matter the amount of wealth you would accumulate or the level of your success.

Lazarus was a beggar whose condition was repulsive to others. His situation was so deplorable that, others had to lay him at the gate of the rich man in order to beg for food. Verse 21 says that Lazarus was not even seeking for the wealth of food at the rich man's table. He sought only that which the rich man would never eat, yet, that was difficult to come by. What he got was dogs licking his sores. But then, both of them died. What we learn here is that death is the destiny of all no matter what you have or do not have and at death, one's destiny is sealed. What is important is to have God as the anchor of your soul.

It is very interesting that Solomon is very concerned about this principle and expressed it as follows:

Then I hated all my labor in which I had toiled under the sun, because I must leave it to the man [Rehoboam] who will come after me. And who knows whether he

*will be wise or a fool? Yet he will rule over all my labor
in which I toiled and in which I have shown myself wise
under the sun. This also is vanity (Ecclesiastes 2:18-19).*

Solomon was concerned about turning dominion, wealth, and all his riches over to his own son because he did not know what would happen. Now, if Solomon who was a man created by God to be a steward of all that belonged to God was so much concerned; do you think that God is going to be any less concerned about turning much greater power and dominion and eternal life over to those who are part of the purpose that He is working out? Do you think that God will be any less concerned when the stakes are so much greater? No, I don't think so. That is why He wants to be involved in our lives to give it a meaning and prepare us for true riches, wealth, power, and dominion that are incomparable and incorruptible.

Solomon could do very little about the situation because he faced death. He was thus powerless over anything that happened after his death. And that is why he said that this is also vanity. There was nothing that he could do about it once he was dead.

God is not without His resources, and He is doing what Solomon should have known and done. He is preparing His children to take care of the dominion that He is going to be giving to them. And so, He will prepare us to rule wisely for His Kingdom. So, he has surrounded us with enough evidence of Himself so that we will recognize His existence, which should move us to seek after Him. As soon as that happens, we become people who are living by higher laws than the laws of this world. Without embracing this fundamental truth no one can reach the potential and live a fulfilled meaningful life.

Lazarus had God in his life and so when he died, he was carried by angels into *Abraham's bosom* while the rich man went to Hades. All the riches of the rich man were vanity, and Solomon's writings also ended on this same note – Ecclesiastes 12:6-8: " *Remember him—before the silver cord is severed, and the golden bowl is broken; before the pitcher is shattered at the spring, and the wheel broken at the well, and the dust returns to the ground it came from, and the spirit returns to God who gave it. "Meaningless! Meaningless!" says the Teacher. "Everything is meaningless!"*

The summary of the Book of Ecclesiastes comes in the very last chapter. Remember God while you're young (Ecclesiastes 12:1), before old age sets in and the teeth give way and the eyes begin to dim (Ecclesiastes 12:3), and the hearing goes bad (Ecclesiastes 12:4). His "end of the matter, after all has been heard" is this, *"Fear God and keep his commandments, for this is the whole duty of man"* (Ecclesiastes 12:13) because it's certain that *"God will bring every deed into judgment, with every secret thing, whether good or evil"* (Ecclesiastes 12:14).

Solomon searched to find the meaning of life. He considers every natural situation that man has experienced. Suddenly, Solomon turns from the natural man to the Spirit man. He finds the answers there. *The only solution to all the questions raised about life and issues are in God.* And the secret to a truly meaningful and successful life is *to fear God and keep His commandments.*

Indeed, Solomon was realistic about life but Jesus knew more. He knew that the darkness Solomon experienced in his life despite everything he had could be turned to light. Nonetheless, in view of the darkness of man and the shortness

97

of life that Solomon described in the book of Ecclesiastes, there is still hope for the Christian even after death- *life beyond death*, as we also see in the parable of the rich man and Lazarus.

Many successful and influential people more often than not also experience Solomon's void and emptiness in life. Even after acquiring all the money and affluence in the world; they still feel a sense of emptiness as though their lives are missing out on something. *That emptiness is a separation between themselves and the Creator of all things.*

Let me bring attention to what was discussed earlier on in Chapter two, that God created mankind in His Own image and gave them two options to enjoy a fulfilled life by trusting and obeying Him but somehow, man made a regrettable mistake by rebelling against God, the Creator. Mankind was then banished from the Garden of Eden – *God's presence*. I see this as a separation between mankind and his Creator.

Adam and Eves' act of disobedience was a repudiation of God's authority over their lives. We refer to their rebellious choice as -*"the fall*," and because they represented all of humanity, their action affects us too. We have, through our attitudes and actions declared ourselves to be God's enemies. In theology, we call it "*original sin.*" This means that human beings are no longer born morally good but are born with an evil inclination to disobey authority. "*Therefore, just as through one-man sin entered the world, and death through sin, and thus death spread to all men, because all sinned*" (Roman 5:12); "*Behold, I was brought forth in iniquity, and in sin my mother conceived me*" (Psalm 51:5).

98

The rebellion of our first parents (Adam and Eve) resulted in physical and spiritual death which affected all. This state of humanity in the fall is "*depravity*" and it talks about humanity's inability to pass the test to please God (The Greek word is "*adokimos*" (see also Romans 1:28; John 5:42; Romans 7:18,23, 8:7; Ephesians. 4:18, 2 Timothy 3:2-4).

Redemption by Christ

Christ's Redemption is a divine key to unlock the doors to a meaningful life. A key element of humanity's depravity is the fact of man's inability to save himself. Naturally, we are alienated from God because of our evil behavior which resulted from our inherited sinful nature (Colossians 1:21). In Romans 3:10, we are informed that, there is no one righteous and neither there is any who seek God. Moving on from verse 13-18, Paul presents an anatomical analysis of man, showing that every organ in the body has become instrument of sin due to our depravity. He says, our throats are a grave, corrupted and defiling, and the tongue is deceitful (verse 13). The lips of man, much like the viper, conceal deadly poison; they are instruments of destruction. The mouth is full of curses and bitter words (verse 14). The feet hasten us to deeds of evil (verse 15).

Morally, every man falls short of the standard of righteousness which God has set. By this we do not mean to say that man cannot do anything that his fellow man considers good. But the Bible teaches that no one will ever be justified (be declared righteous), by his works because by the works of the Law no flesh will be justified in His sight for through the Law comes the knowledge of sin (Romans 3:20). This also means we were by nature the objects of wrath – (Ephesians. 2:3).

This is very serious because if God does not save us, we will be lost forever and life in this world would be meaningless no matter how successful one's life may be. Living a life that is totally separated from God, your creator is meaningless and it is this separation that creates a sense of emptiness and void in peoples' lives no matter the level of their achievement in life. Remember the 5 questions we considered in Chapter 6 of this book: *Who am I? Where am I from? Why am I here? What can I do? and where am I going?*

After the fall of man, God, the loving Creator, who shows Himself to be wrathful toward our sin is determined to turn evil and suffering we have caused into good that will be to His ultimate glory. So, the next movement shows God implementing a *master plan* for redeeming this world by rescuing fallen sinners through Jesus Christ. Let us see how God did this:

> *For when we were still without strength, in due time Christ died for the ungodly. For scarcely for a righteous man will one die; yet perhaps for a good man someone would even dare to die. But God demonstrates His own love toward us, in that while we were still sinners, Christ died for us. Much more then, having now been justified by His blood, we shall be saved from wrath through Him. For if when we were enemies we were reconciled to God through the death of His Son, much more, having been reconciled, we shall be saved by His life (Romans 5:6-10).*

So, when Jesus was born (incarnated), it was God Himself who had come to renew the world and restore His people. The grand narrative of Scripture climaxes with the death and resurrection of Jesus to bring salvation to humanity. The question is: *What about those who lived before Christ was born?* One may ask. Now, reading the Bible, there are several typologies of God's redemptive acts all of which find their fulfilment in Christ Jesus.

Let us consider some few examples in the Old Testament: *One*, in the beginning when Adam and Eve sinned as recorded in the book of Genesis, God mentioned that *"the seed of the woman"* would crush the head of the serpent that deceived them. By this, he was pointing to Jesus. Man was naked and so God covered Adam and Eve's nakedness. *Why did He do that?* He was pointing to the redemptive work of Christ.

Two, when the sins of man had increased and the earth had to be destroyed at the time with flood, he placed Noah in the ark; and *three*, when he caused Abraham into deep sleep, established his covenant with him, and when he asked for the sacrifice of Isaac, he was pointing to Jesus Christ. *Four*, the redemption of Israel from Egypt prefigured Christ's redemption, the Levitical system of priesthood and the temple rituals all pointed to Jesus, and the list can go on and on.

In the New Testament, Paul writes: *"When the fullness of time had come,"* when the moment was appropriate in God's plan, *"God sent forth his Son, born of woman, born under the law, to redeem those who were under the law"* (Galatians 4:4–5). The coming of Christ and His work on earth, especially his crucifixion and resurrection should not be an afterthought of God but rather His foreknowledge, which He foreordained.

More importantly the climax of history. This is the great turning point at which God accomplished the salvation throughout history. So, *whiles the past age looked forward to Christ's redemptive work, the present age looks back on Christ's completed work.*

Jesus has accomplished God's redemptive work for humanity and all who entrust Him with their lives are saved. *Your sins are forgiven;* the penalty of sin which is death has been cancelled. You have been reconciled to God- your creator, and you can enjoy life in its eternity. Let us consider what Jesus said on the cross where all this was made possible:

> *Later, knowing that everything had now been finished, and so that Scripture would be fulfilled, Jesus said, "I am thirsty." A jar of wine vinegar was there, so they soaked a sponge in it, put the sponge on a stalk of the hyssop plant, and lifted it to Jesus' lips. When he had received the drink, Jesus said, "It is finished." With that, he bowed his head and gave up his spirit (John 19:28-30).*

The significance of Jesus' last statement before his death on the cross: "*It is finished*" is the English translation of the Greek word- *Tetelestai;* which comes from the verb *teleo,* meaning "*to bring to an end, to complete, or to accomplish*". This word is key to giving Christians the meaning to living a triumphant life here on earth because it marks the end of a particular course of action, which is: a life of *endless* toil, struggles, pains, diseases, suffering and sorrows.

Tetelestai is in the perfect tense in Greek, which presupposes that the word is an action word which has been completed in the past with results continuing into the present. It is different from the past tense which only looks back to an event. When Jesus cried out "*It is finished*," He meant "*It was finished in the past, it is still finished in the present, and it will remain finished in the future*." Hallelujah! There's no reason for you to panic and be afraid of what may happen tomorrow. When Jesus died, he left no unfinished business behind. This has actually given more value to life because it has saved us from sin and the power of sin; bringing us into alignment with God so we will know His will and live for His purpose to restore immortality to our lives.

God's Testimony About Life

> *And this is the testimony: God has given us eternal life, and this life is in his Son. Whoever has the Son has life; whoever does not have the Son of God does not have life. I write these things to you who believe in the name of the Son of God so that you may know that you have eternal life (1 John 5:11-13).*

The Christian's life is secured in Christ Jesus and therefore there is no need for the believer to be afraid of the many difficulties and challenges this world presents because: "*For you died, and your life is now hidden with Christ in God. When Christ, who is your life, appears, then you also will appear with him in glory*" (Colossians 3:3-4). From the Scriptures above, it is evident that Christ Jesus is our life and so the life of a Christian needs not follow after the pattern of unbelievers. The enemy, who is Satan has been defeated by Christ; and therefore, we are at liberty to live life to the fullest, without fear of sicknesses, diseases, storms, and all the other fears of life. Christ has given us a glorious future which gives meaning to our present life. *"For I consider that the sufferings of this present time are not worthy to be compared with the glory which shall be revealed in us"* (Romans 8:18).

True fulfilment and life's meaning come from knowing God and walking with Him faithfully. When that happens, He shows us each step to take daily to live victoriously and approach life with confidence. Solomon observed that the Lord has a perfect plan for each of us; nevertheless, he allows us to make our own choices. Therefore, we are unaware of His big-picture or plan; rather we wrestle with His moral preferences at every decision-point. Submit your will to the Lord. Don't be like Solomon who recounted all the foolish decisions he made as a result of turning away from the true God who alone can give our lives meaning. *"Though no one can go back and make a brand-new start, anyone can start from now and make a brand-new ending." - Carl Bard* (Retrieved from https://www.pinterest.com-accessed on 08/17/2019).

CHAPTER TEN

THE SEASONS OF LIFE

•

Times and seasons are a regular part of life, no matter where you live. Before mankind was created, God established times and seasons as a basic part of our universe. Let us listen to God in time past *"Then God said, "Let there be lights in the firmament of the heavens to divide the day from the night; and let them be for signs and seasons, and for days and years"* (Genesis 1:14). God has established seasons and times to accomplish His will. Beyond these specific calendar seasons, are other large sections of a year like hunting season, football season, and holy day or holiday seasons.

Times and seasons contemplate working in harmony with nature to make life more profitable. As a result, Solomon in search for meaning in life realized that: *"To everything there is a season, a time for every purpose under heaven"* (Ecclesiastes 3:1). The import of what Solomon is saying here is that there is a season for everything and a time for every purpose - this means seasons and times influence what is done and the right purpose.

From birth to the moment of our death, God is accomplishing His divine purposes; even though, we do not always understand what He is doing in our lives. You do not need to be a philosopher or a scientist to know that times *and seasons* are regular part of life irrespective of location. If it had not been for the dependability of God-ordained *natural laws*, daily living would have been chaotic, if not impossible. For that reason, not only are there times and seasons in this world but also there is an overruling providence in our lives. The following Bible verses from the book of Ecclesiastes support the concept of time, as follows: Ecclesiastes 3:1-8; Ecclesiastes 3:2; Ecclesiastes 3:3; Ecclesiastes 3:5; Ecclesiastes 3:6; and Ecclesiastes 3:7). Look Up: God Orders Time (Ecclesiastes 3:1-8)

While the earth's rotation around the sun provides *day* and *night*; the apparent movement of the sun (revolution of the earth) provides the four seasons- *winter, spring, summer,* and *fall*. This is validated by God's promise to Noah: *"As long as the world exists, there will be a time for planting and a time for harvest. There will always be cold and heat, summer and winter, day and night"* (Genesis 8:22, GNT). Likewise, Solomon goes on to enumerate *twenty-eight* activities; as follows:

> *A time to be born, and a time to die; a time to plant, and a time to pluck what is planted; A time to kill, and a time to heal; a time to break down, and a time to build up; A time to weep, and a time to laugh; a time to mourn, and a time to dance; A time to cast away stones, and a time to gather stones; a time to embrace, and a time to refrain from embracing; A time to gain, and a time to lose; a time to keep, and a time to throw away;*

*A time to tear, and a time to sew; a time to keep silence,
and a time to speak; A time to love, and a time to hate;
a time of war, and a time of peace (Ecclesiastes 3:2-8)*

What Solomon is saying is that providence arranges the moment for everything to happen in human affairs, including the duration of its operation and the appropriate time. There is the urgent need to cooperate with God to know His divine purpose and to know His intentions, else we labor for nothing. The Bible is emphatic as follows: *"What profit has the worker from that in which he labors? I have seen the God-given task with which the sons of men are to be occupied"* (Ecclesiastes 3:9-10). In his contribution to the discussion, Matthew Henry, commenting on Ecclesiastes 3:1-10 asserted:

> *To expect unchanging happiness in a changing world,
> must end in disappointment. To bring ourselves to our
> state in life, is our duty and wisdom in this world. God's
> whole plan for the government of the world will be
> found altogether wise, just, and good. Then let us seize
> the favorable opportunity for every good purpose and
> work. The time to die is fast approaching. Thus, labor
> and sorrow fill the world. This is given us, that we may
> always have something to do; none were sent into the
> world to be idle (May 1998, 1991, p.819).*

The believer is to seek God to direct his or her paths in wisdom to do the right thing at the right time, and this can be achieved when we are identified as stewards of God's gracious gift; and for this reason, Solomon was a man blessed by God to fulfil divine assignment. Solomon had to wait patiently for God to fulfil His promise in his life because it could be futile to operate outside of God's will, purpose, and timing. Consequently, a wise man, Solomon advises, as follows: *"I returned and saw under the sun that the race is not to the swift, nor the battle to the strong, nor bread to the wise, nor riches to men of understanding, nor favor to men of skill; But time and chance happen to them all"* (Ecclesiastes 9:11).

Let us consider a season of life before he was made king of Israel. Solomon, as a child did not know what will happen to him in adulthood, yet God had chosen him over his elder brother (Adonijah) to succeed his father (1Chronicles 17and 28). However, prior to David's death, Adonijah had declared himself king over Israel against God's plan and purpose (1Kings 1).

Whatever God does is good and his timing is perfect. Therefore, if we co-operate with God's timing, life will not be meaningless; because everything will be *"beautiful in His time"* including the most difficult experiences of life. Arguably, there is *a time to pluck what is planted; A time to kill, and a time to heal; a time to break down, and a time to build up ...."* I have good news for you, if God has set eternity in the heart of men; then, death is not the end of life.

You may ask: *What must be done in life before death dawns on me?* If this is your question, I wish to point to what Solomon said at the end of his research.

First, *look within: Eternity is in your heart* - The supreme purpose of all human activities is what Solomon talks about times and seasons in life, which begins with birth and death. Well, let us find out: *"A time to be born, and a time to die."* As a result, birth and death are not human accidents, but divine appointments because God is in control. Ponder over Psalm 139:13-16, which stipulates that God has so woven us in the womb with a genetic structure; perfect for the work He has prepared for us. Nevertheless, of all the seasons of life, birth and death are to be viewed as the opening and closing of mankind's time on earth.

All other seasons are sandwiched between the two. Even though, life is not supposed to terminate at death because God has set eternity in the hearts of men. For this reason, what happens to man after death is determined by what one does with his or her life.

Second, *life on earth is a season for preparation*- What we need to understand in this chapter is that, *life, death*, and *eternity* are the *"ingredients"* that make up the experiences of man in this world; and as a result, these variables must not be ignored. Throughout his writings, Solomon repeatedly mentions the certainty of death (see also Ecclesiastes 2:16; 3:20; 5:15-16; 6:6; 8:8; 9:2-3,12; and 12:7-8). The Bible states that death is inevitable, and judgement comes after death (Hebrews 9:18).

In *fourteen statements* but discussed under *seven themes*, Solomon affirms God's work in our individual lives, seeking to accomplish His will in mankind. All the events come from God and rooted in time. As a result, the inference is plain: *if we cooperate with God's timing, life will not be meaningless.* Everything will be *beautiful in His time* (verse 11), including the most difficult experiences of life.

Most of the statements are easy to understand so we will examine only those that may need special explanation.

One: *birth and death* (verse 2) - As established earlier, birth and death are not human accidents; but should be viewed as divine appointments. God has prepared a time when we enter upon scenes of life to incur the obligation of duty. The moment we take our part in this system of providence, we become eligible for another great event, determined by the Divine decree – Death. (Read Genesis 29:31-30:24; Joshua 24:3; 1 Samuel 1:9-20; Psalm 113:9 and 127; Jeremiah 1:4-5; Luke 1:5-25; Galatians 1:15 and 4:4). Even though, things like abortion, birth control, mercy killing, and surrogate parenthood make it look as though man is in control of birth and death, but Solomon states otherwise. By way of illustration, Psalm 139:13-16 can be contradicted (read also Ephesians 2:10); yet man can foolishly hasten his or her death, but we cannot prevent it when our time comes, unless God so wills it (Isaiah 38). Consequently, *"all the days ordained for me were written in Your book"* (Psalm 139:16, NIV). Like Job, we need a heart of wisdom to number our days.

Two: *planting and plucking* (verse 2)- The Jews appreciated the seasons because they were agricultural people, whose religious calendar was based on the agricultural year (Leviticus 23). They understood this principle very well; you cannot plug when you have not planted. Yet, men may plough and sow, but only God can give the increase (Psalm 65:9-13). *Plucking* may refer to either: (i) reaping or pulling up unproductive plants. A successful farmer must know that nature can work for him only if (s)he works with nature. *This is also the secret of a successful life: learn God's principles and cooperate with them.*

Three: *killing and healing* (verse 3)- This probably refers, not to war (verse 8) or self-defence; but to the results of sickness

110

and plague in the land (1 Samuel 2:6). While God permits some to die, others are healed; but this does not imply that we should refuse medical aid because God can use modern medicine, as well as, miracles to accomplish His purposes (Isaiah 38).

Solomon does not present these details from a moral point of view, the time here is not that which is morally right, but that which, be it morally right or not, has been determined by God, the Governor of the world and Former of history, who makes even that which is evil subservient to His plan. Watch closely the contrast between the striking down of life and the salvation of an endangered life by healing; this is what God is doing in our lives. Our time hear on earth is a season for healing, provided for, by God through the Salvation offered by Jesus Christ. The fact is, by the entrance of sin, mankind is bound under the power of Satan, but Jesus has come that we shall be free. Sin and Satan were to be destroyed; and Christ triumphed over them on his cross. But the children of men, who stand out against these offers, shall be dealt with as enemies. Christ was to be the Saviour and Comforter, and so he is; he is sent to give life to those who are dead in sin and comfort all who mourn, that they may abound in the fruits of righteousness, as the branches of God's planting. Neither the mercy of God, the atonement of Christ, nor the gospel of grace, profit the self-sufficient and proud. What we need to do, is to accept God's offer of Salvation and be healed of the sin disease before the day of trouble.

In his contribution to the discussion, Adam Clarke's, commenting on Ecclesiastes 3:3 asserted: *"The healing art, when out of season used, Pernicious proves, and serves to hasten death. But timely medicines drooping nature raise, and health restore. -Now, Justice wields her sword with wholesome rigour, nor the offender spares: But Mercy now is more expedient found. On crazy fabrics ill-timed cost bestowed. No purpose answers, when discretion bids to pull them down, and wait a season fit to build anew." (1996, 2003, 2005, 2006 by Biblesoft, Inc.)*

Four: *casting away stones and gathering stones* (verse 5)- Stones are neither good nor bad; it all depends on what you do with them. People gathered stones for building walls and houses. Therefore, build something out of them! *Tour guides* in Israel will tell you that God gave stones to an angel and told him to distribute them across the world and he tripped right over Palestine! It is indeed a rocky land and farmers must clear their fields before they can plow and plant. As a result, if one wants to hurt an enemy, one fills up his field with stones (2 Kings 3:19, 25). I argue that if your enemy fills your land with rocks, don't throw them back. You should rather use it to build something profitable.

I believe these words describe destruction and rebuilding, and suggest to us that, human monuments cannot endure forever; each age requires a new embodiment of truth. Hence the necessity of current literature. From the time of the fall of man in the beginning, mankind has sought to rely on so many things to make life meaningful and fulfilling. Things like wisdom, knowledge, power, material things and many others. But history shows that, these things always give way for new ones yet, we are not fulfilled. What we need is God and His word. Our lives here are like building a house and if we use any material apart from the word of God, the house will one day crumble down (Luke 6:46-49).

God is building a new house with new stones

From the time Israel failed and God expressed his discontent in them (Isaiah 5:2-5), He started gathering new stones to build a spiritual house, a holy priesthood, to offer spiritual sacrifices acceptable to God through Jesus Christ (1Peter 2:4-8).

I believe Solomon spoke prophetically when he wrote this; that man-made religion and self-effort will be rejected by God and then God will build His Own house. Jesus spoke about this in Matthew chapter 23 *"O Jerusalem, Jerusalem, the one who kills the prophets and stones those who are sent to her! How often I wanted to gather your children together, as a hen gathers her chicks under her wings, but you were not willing! See! Your house is left to you desolate; for I say to you, you shall see Me no more till you say, 'Blessed is He who comes in the name of the Lord!'" (Matthew 23:37-39)*

When men forsake God and begin to gather their own stones, God forsakes them. We are created in the image of God to be a temple for God but when we reach a stage of corruption, the time for scattering stones is not far off. This is what has happened to humanity but thank God for His work of redemption through Jesus Christ.

We are in a season where God is gathering living stones for His spiritual building, and the Gentiles, once cast-away stones, have in due time, been made part of the spiritual building (Eph. 2:19-20), and children of Abraham (Matt 3:9); so, the restored Jews hereafter (Ps 102:13-14; Zech. 9:16).

My question to you is, are you part of what God is doing?

Do not wait until it is too late, you can become a living stone in the hands of God; come to Jesus the living stone, though rejected by men, but chosen by God and precious. Now is the time; be part of what God is doing.

Five: embracing and refraining from embracing (verse 5)- People in the Near East openly show affection such as kissing and hugging when meeting or when parting company. So, this could be restated as: *"A time to say hello and a time to say good-bye"* Furthermore, everybody needs to be loved and accepted. But there is a time when affection and acceptance are difficult to access. A bosom friend may turn cynical and hollow-hearted. Sometimes we refrain from embracing because our embrace is not reciprocated but the love, we receive from God is unconditional. It is always receiving and never rejects.

Six: getting and losing (verse 6) or *"a time to search and a time to give it up for lost"* is another translation. The next phrase gives biblical authority for garage sales: *a time to keep and a time to clean the house*! Humans have the tendency for holding on to things, even when those things have outlived their purpose. To make life meaningful, you should learn how to let things go.

Lastly, tearing and mending (verse 7)- This probably refers to the Jewish practice of tearing one's garments during a time of grief or repentance (2 Samuel 13:31; Ezra 9: 5). God expects us to grieve during bereavement, yet unlike unbelievers (1 Thessalonians 4:13-18). There comes a time when we must get out the needle and thread to start sewing things up!

Please return to Ecclesiastes 12:

114

Remember now your Creator in the days of your youth,
before the difficult days come, and the years draw near
when you say, "I have no pleasure in them": While
the sun and the light, the moon and the stars, are not
darkened, and the clouds do not return after the rain; In
the day when the keepers of the house tremble, and the
strong men bow down; when the grinders cease because
they are few, and those that look through the windows
grow dim; When the doors are shut in the streets, and
the sound of grinding is low; When one rises up at
the sound of a bird, and all the daughters of music
are brought low. Also they are afraid of height, and of
terrors in the way; when the almond tree blossoms, the
grasshopper is a burden, and desire fails. For man goes to
his eternal home, and the mourners go about the streets.
Remember your Creator before the silver cord is loosed,
or the golden bowl is broken, or the pitcher shattered at
the fountain, or the wheel broken at the well. Then the
dust will return to the earth as it was, and the spirit will
return to God who gave it. "Vanity of vanities," says the
Preacher,
"All is vanity." And moreover, because the Preacher
was wise, he still taught the people knowledge; yes, he
pondered and sought out and set in order many proverbs.
The Preacher sought to find acceptable words; and what
was written was upright—words of truth. The words of
the wise are like goads, and the words of scholars are like
well-driven nails, given by one Shepherd. And further,
my son, be admonished by these. Of making many books
there is no end, and much study is wearisome to the
flesh. Let us hear the conclusion of the whole matter:

Fear God and keep His commandments, for this is man's all. For God will bring every work into judgment, including every secret thing, whether good or evil (Ecclesiastes 12:1-14).

What we have learned in this chapter is that God by his providence governs the world, and has determined particular things and operations to particular times. In those times such things may be done with propriety and success; but if we neglect the appointed seasons, we sin against this providence, and become the authors of our own distresses. The truth is, the seasons and times are authentic in that there is no mistake about them, just like what a symphony ought to be. Indeed, from birth to death, God is accomplishing His divine purposes; even though, we do not always appear to understand what He is doing. For that reason, Solomon helps us to have a peak into what God is doing in this life by suggesting that: *"He has made everything beautiful in its time. Also, He has put eternity in their hearts, except that no one can find out the work that God does from beginning to end."* That is why we need Him.

CHAPTER ELEVEN

❖

LIVING ABUNDANT LIFE

•

Many people have the belief that, "life is too short, so we must enjoy it." To them, the Christian life is boring. Christians of every stripe *the world* over are thought to be dull, humorless, austere people. Many Christians today are ridiculed by the world on some social media platforms because they practice modest lifestyles and preach against unrestrained hedonism. It is a common misconception among non-Christians that the Christian life is frankly, boring. *Have you ever been referred to as being boring or out of touch?*

Modern mainline Protestants have tried to shed this *"not cool"* image. Today, many churches hold contemporary services to replace or add to the traditional service. This has culminated into modern and pop-culture service; featuring live, upbeat music, extensive use of pictures and computer graphics flashed on huge screens. Another characteristic is the short *sermons* given by high-energy youth pastors; with mostly young attendees, who wear casual clothes ranging from blue jeans and *T-shirts* to *khakis,* and polo shirts. This change in *format* has been a conscious choice aimed at ridding Christianity of its apparent dreary reputation among the *unchurched.* Even so, if the world considers unrestrained pleasure-seeking as the norm in terms of *fun* and *living large;* Biblical Christianity will indeed be considered lackluster and unyielding by comparison.

A Christian no longer should live the rest of his time in the flesh for the lusts of the world and in pleasure seeking, instead for the will of God. For we have spent precious time in the past to gratify the desires of the flesh; when we walked in lewdness, lusts, drunkenness, revelries, drinking parties, and abominable idolatries. Yet, we found no fulfilment in them. No matter how deep one was involved, there was still the feeling of void and emptiness in life. Then, you turn to Christ by His grace and the world thinks it is strange that you do not run with them in the same flood of dissipation and end up speaking evil of you (I Peter 4:2-4).

Dear reader, I wish to remind you that by just exercising self-control as a child of God, does not mean your life is boring, underprivileged, and unrewarding. In fact, when lived properly, the Christian life is ultimately more exciting, successful, and satisfying than most human beings can imagine! Certainly, the lives of Christians are full of responsibility and self-restraint, but the rewards and blessings that accrue over a lifetime of pleasing God and living His way of life simply overwhelm the seemingly onerous duties and strictures. There is no comparison!

Most people are not aware that this is a primary reason Christ came as a man to this earth—to *teach us how to live abundant and fulfilled lives*. Notice His plain statement recorded by John in his gospel account: *"I have come that they [His sheep, Christians] may have life, and that they may have it more abundantly."* (John 10:10). The Bible is clear in its calls for Christians to cease behaving as most people in the world do, by implication: *"I have come that they may have life, and that they may have it more abundantly"* (John 10:10).

What Is Abundant Life?

According to the very Founder of Christianity, His disciples; if they follow His teachings will live enviable and full lives! *They will have lives worth living*! But, specifically, what does He mean by *"life . . . more abundantly"? What is abundant life?* A problem arises when discussing this concept due to the apparent subjectivity of the term- *"abundant."* What is abundant living for one person may be absolutely unsatisfying for another. A hard-charging, A-type businessman, who is into exotic vacations, sports cars, and rock climbing would not consider a rocking chair on the porch, a vegetable garden at the back of the house, and a weekly round of golf at the local course to be fulfilling; yet they would probably suit a retired senior citizen just fine. *One person's bowl of cherries is another's bowl of cherry pits.*

Across five studies conducted in the United States of America, conservatives have reported greater purpose and meaning in life than liberals at each reporting period (Newman, Schwarz, Graham, & Stone, 2018). The findings remain significant after adjusting for religiosity and were usually stronger than the association involving other well-being measures (Newman,

Schwarz, Graham, & Stone, 2018). The fact is, when we come to Christ, we have entrusted our lives to God who is able to do exceedingly abundantly above all that we ask or think (Ephesians 3:20). Likewise, the meaning of life is more linked to social conservatism than economic conservatism (Newman, Schwarz, Graham, & Stone, 2018).

The Greek word Jesus uses in John 10:10 to describe the kind of life He came to teach humanity, is *perissón*, meaning *"superabundant," "superfluous," "overflowing," "over and above a certain quantity," "a quantity so abundant as to be considerably more than what one would expect or anticipate."* In short, He promises us a life far better than we could ever envision, reminiscent of I Corinthians 2:9, *"Eye has not seen, nor ear heard, nor have entered into the heart of man the things which God has prepared for those who love Him"*. However, before we begin to have imaginations of palatial homes, classic automobiles, *around-the-world* trips, and wads of pocket money, we need to step back and consider what *God* says about *"life."*

The human idea of wealth, prestige, position, and power in this world are not high-priority items on God's list of blessings, and so, they do not necessarily define life. In His statement-*that they may have life … have it more abundantly*; Jesus affirms that one is not only saved on believing on Him but also such a person will enjoy the fullness of life on earth. Similarly, God supplies those who believe in Him with the needed strength and power to live God's way. Reflect on this passage: *"His divine power has given us all things pertaining to life and godliness through the knowledge f Him who has called us to glory and virtue"* (2 Peter 1:3). For that reason, *"And this is* eternal life, that they may know You, the only true God, and Jesus Christ whom You have sent" (John 17:3).

What can we take from this? **Abundant life**, the kind of life in which all people must truly be interested in, is not determined by accumulation of wealth but through a relationship with God. *Abundant life*—the life God offers us through Jesus Christ and His teaching—is thus about *quality*, not quantity. Put another way, the *abundant life* is life as God lives it; for once, we truly come to know God we cultivate the desire to emulate Him. Again, let me bring our minds back to the Bible passages we read (John 17:3 and 2 Peter 1:3); we realize that they do not make mention of length of days, health, prosperity, family, occupation, and many more—*in fact*, the only meaning is *knowing God*!

Material blessings; though good, and I argue that believers will want them; yet may or may not be *by-products* of God's way of life, Likewise, neither our wealth nor poverty is an indication of our standing with God. Nevertheless, God desires that we *"prosper in all things and be in good health"* (3 John 2), but the bottom line is, we need to know God and walk in truth and not necessarily living like royalty. The Bible declares: *"I have no greater joy than to hear that my children walk in truth"* (3 John 4) .

I am by no means suggesting that material blessings and accumulation of wealth is bad. In fact, the Bible is full of promises of prosperity and material wealth but still Jesus in His teaching, shifted the focus to the prosperity of the Soul. Metz (2015) offered: *"I hereby aim to enrich reflection about what it is about the lives of Nelson Mandela, Mother Teresa, Albert Einstein, and Pablo Picasso that made them so significant*

121

as well as to indicate how fundamentality implicitly plays a key role in theistic conceptions of meaning in life" As humans, we are naturally oriented toward material things; however, as Christians, our perspective must change. After all, Paul admonishes, *"Set your mind on things above, not on things on the earth. For you died [in baptism], and your life is hidden with Christ in God"* (Colossians 3:2-3).

King Solomon lived a similar life of wealth, power, and privilege. I mentioned in the previous Chapters how he attempted to find fulfilment in his wealth, wisdom, possessions, hobbies, and creature comforts. *What does he ultimately conclude about how humanity should live?* Here is a vivid answer to the way humans should live; thus says the Lord: *"Let not the wise man glory in his wisdom, Let not the mighty man glory in his might, Nor let the rich man glory in his riches; But let him who glories glory in this, That he understands and knows Me, That I am the Lord, exercising lovingkindness, judgment, and righteousness in the earth. For in these I delight,"says the Lord"* (Jeremiah 9:23-24).

So, what we need to understand is that God's provisions are revelations of the provider and not the provisions; this is to say that, when God blesses us, they are to lead us to acknowledge Him and honor Him above what we have been blessed with. Ponder over this scripture: *"For what will it profit a man if he gains the whole world, and loses his own soul? Or what will a man give in exchange for his soul?"* (Mark 8:36-37). Remember Job, a man who was blessed by God to become the greatest of all the people of the East (Job 1:1-3). Even Satan testified about him saying the Lord has *"blessed the work of his hands, and his possessions have increased in the land"* (verse 10).

Job lost all his possessions within a short period of time but he remained content and grateful to God despite the loss. He understood that, *knowing God was of more value and fulfilling than having all of the world's riches without God.* Likewise, he knew that God was the source of all that he possessed and they could not take the place of God in his life. I am challenged by his reaction to his loss of possessions including his sons and daughters, as follows- "Then Job arose, tore his robe, and shaved his head; and he fell to the ground and worshiped. And he said: *"Naked I came from my mother's womb, and naked shall I return there. The Lord gave, and the Lord has taken away; Blessed be the name of the Lord." In all this Job did not sin nor charge God with wrong"* (Job 1:20-22).

His conclusion is totally compatible with Jesus' statement in John 10:10. Jesus did not come promising us wealth, prestige, and pleasure on earth. Although He does promise us these things in the world to come, and we may enjoy them now when we place faith in Him, the good news He presents is about how to attain eternal life (John 6:40). Like Solomon's, His message is very clear, *". . . if you want to enter into life, know God and His Son Jesus Christ and then keep His commandments"* (Matthew 19:17). Remember now your Creator in the days of your youth before the difficult days come. . . . Fear God and keep His commandments, for this is the whole duty of man. For God will bring every work into judgment, including every secret thing, whether it is good or whether it is evil. (Ecclesiastes 12:1, 13-14).

The insight is that *abundant life* is implicit in knowing God and His Son Jesus Christ; as well as, keeping God's commandments, in tandem with the grace that is supplied through Jesus Christ. Therefore, Jesus came to reconcile man to God and to give man the means by which he could properly keep God's commandments; and as a result, His grace puts commandment-keeping in its proper place. Once a person lives this way, what Apostle Paul calls "*walking in the Spirit*" (Galatians 5:16-25); he is naturally going to experience abundant life because he is no longer under the penalties and curses that the infraction of the law exacts (see also verse 18). As a result, his life will be pleasing unto God to enable God to bless him now and in the life to come (Psalm 19:8-11; Proverbs 11:18-20; and Matthew 6:33).

A solid relationship with our Creator is *the key* to abundant life; for there is no greater and satisfying accomplishment than knowing Jesus Christ, as well as, appreciating that Jesus is living His life through you. When we reach this point of realization, we would have learned the godly perspective of living in abundant life. Moreover, if we see spiritual growth taking place in our lives, including the production of good fruit in our lives, we experience the results of a strengthened relationship with God. I pose these questions: *Are you living abundant lives? Are you reaping the rewards of following God's way of life? Have you begun to enjoy the benefits of keeping God's commandments?*

CONCLUSION

This book is aimed at shedding light on: "*The Meaning of Life*" based on the Biblical account of King Solomon in the book of Ecclesiastes. The questions addressed in the book are *two-fold,* as follows: (1) *What is life about? a*nd (2) w*hat is the meaningfulness of life with or without God?*

These questions were addressed using eleven themes: What is Life (1), the concept of life (chapter 2), the choices we make that tend to become life (chapter 3); and chapter 4 covered the responsibility of God. The profitability of God was discussed under chapter 5. Additionally, the fear of God was treated in chapter 6, followed by how to figure it all out (chapter 7), there is nothing new under the sun (chapter 8), Christ gives meaning to life (chapter 9); and in chapters 10 and 11, the seasons of life and living abundant life are respectively treated.

I posed the question: *Has life seemed monotonous and meaningless to you?* Well, it needs not be because life is a tremendous blessing from God to mankind. The three-best scholarship (Jeffrey Meyers, Michael Eaton, Sidney Greidanus) on Ecclesiastes-have summed up the book as follows: **first**- "*defends the life of faith in a generous God by pointing to the grimness of the alternative*" (Michael Eaton); **second**, "*true wisdom*" ... "*is to fear God and keep his commandments, to receive and use the gifts of God with joy and gratitude*" (Jeffrey

Meyers); and **three**, *"fear God in order to turn a vain, empty life into a meaningful life which will enjoy God's gifts"* (Sidney Greidanus-O'Donnell, 2014, p.10).

We must accept the reality, though, that we must live by faith in God's promises. Following His resurrection, Jesus says, *"Blessed are those who have not seen, and yet have believed"* (John 20:29). Jesus Christ is *"the power of God, and the wisdom of God"* (I Corinthians 1:24). In His mercy, He has miraculously broken into our lives to prepare us for His Kingdom. We must take up the challenges we are presented with and cease living our lives in circles, rather head straight for the Kingdom of God.

We have the work of Jesus as emphasized by the Gospel of John and the work of Jesus is also remembered through the Lord's supper, Easter celebrations, and many more (O'Donnell, 2014, pp.27-28). **The real answer is in Matthew 6:19-34:**

Do not store up for yourselves treasures on earth, where moths and vermin destroy, and where thieves break in and steal. But store up for yourselves treasures in heaven, where moths and vermin do not destroy, and where thieves do not break in and steal. For where your treasure is, there your heart will be also. "The eye is the lamp of the body. If your eyes are healthy, your whole body will be full of light. But if your eyes are unhealthy, your whole body will be full of darkness. If then the light within you is darkness, how great is that darkness! "No one can serve two masters. Either you will hate the one and love the other, or you will be devoted to the one and despise the other. You cannot serve both God and money.

Do not worry "*Therefore I tell you, do not worry about your life, what you will eat or drink; or about your body, what you will wear. Is not life more than food, and the body more than clothes? Look at the birds of the air; they do not sow or reap or store away in barns, and yet your heavenly Father feeds them. Are you not much more valuable than they? Can any one of you by worrying add a single hour to your life? "And why do you worry about clothes? See how the flowers of the field grow. They do not labor or spin. Yet I tell you that not even Solomon in all his splendor was dressed like one of these. If that is how God clothes the grass of the field, which is here today, and tomorrow is thrown into the fire, will he not much more clothe you—you of little faith?*

So, do not worry, saying, 'What shall we eat?' or 'What shall we drink?' or 'what shall we wear? For the pagans run after all these things, and your heavenly Father knows that you need them. But seek first his kingdom and his righteousness, and all these things will be given to you as well. Therefore, do not worry about tomorrow, for tomorrow will worry about itself. Each day has enough trouble of its own.

The above passage admonishes Christians: (i) *not to store up* and (ii) *not to worry;* because earthly treasures are but passing things- they are here today and tomorrow they are not. Anybody who builds his or her life around them becomes a victim of passing things. Likewise, life under the sun is full of worry and sorrow. What man needs is the kingdom of God, which according to Jesus in John 18:36 is not of this world. We all need the rule of God in our hearts; and this should be our supreme focus whiles we live here on earth. This is what makes life under the sun meaningful in that it prepares you for eternity. Let us finish with II Peter 1:

> *Grace and peace be multiplied to you in the knowledge of God and of Jesus our Lord, as His divine power has given to us all things [everything] that pertains to [eternal] life and godliness, through the knowledge of Him [the Word of God] who called us by glory and virtue, by which have been given to us exceedingly great and precious promises [of Abraham], that through these you may be partakers of the divine nature, having escaped the corruption that is in the world through lust (II Peter 1:2-4).*

Perhaps, the most important thing in these verses for the purpose of this book, is *"His divine power has given to us all things that pertain to life, and godliness, that you have been made partakers of the divine nature"* Connect this to Genesis 1:26. Are we made after the God-kind, or not? So, what is our awesome potential for the future? You know what it is? It is quite simple but so logical.

The study of the book of Ecclesiastes is concentrated not on literary structure, intertextuality, or origins but on meaning; and for that reason, meaning that calls for bringing to bear the sources of wisdom to which our own and other traditions are relevant (Swami, 2015).

From what is given in Scripture, we were created in the image of God to serve His divine purpose. Though we lost that through bad choices, we are now born of God. If we make the right decision to accept Christ into our lives, our God-like image is restored to us; and with that contemplates the responsibility of reflecting Christ in whatever we do here on earth. What is more? We have an inheritance of the promises, and a greatly expanded dominion that will be given us at the end of time. This is what makes life meaningful.

To God be the Glory!

REFERENCES

Battista, J. & Almond, R. (1973). The development of meaning in life. *Interpersonal and Biological Processes, 36*(4), 409-427.doi:10.1 080/00332747.19736.11023774

Bertrand, R. (1946), *Epicureanism: A History of Western Philosophy.* New York, NY: Simon and Schuster; London, United Kingdom: George Allen and Unwin).

Deng, X. (2011). On the problem of the meaning of life in "Chinese Philosophy" *Frontiers of Philosophy in China.6*(4), 608-627. Retrieved from http://www.jstor.org-accessed on 09/21/2019

Denning, K. (February 2011). *Is life what we make of it?* Mathematical, Physical, and Engineering Sciences.doi:10.1098/ rsta.2010.0230

Domino, B. (2012). Looking at the meaning of life Hydra-Scopically: Diderot and the value of the human. *Philosophy and Literature,36*(2), 363-377.doi:10.1353/phl.2012.0022

Griffith J. (2016). *The book of real answers to everything*, World Transformation Movement.p.70.

Harney, M. (2015). *Naturalizing phenomenology-A philosophical imperative.* In Integral Biomathics: Life Sciences, Mathematics, and Phenomenological Philosophy, Process in Biophysics and Molecular Biology,119(3),661-669. doi:10.1016/j. pbiomolbio.2015.08. 005

Islamic Pamphlets (2006). What is the purpose of life? Retrieved from islamicpamphlets.com-accessed on 09/26/2019

Jeffrey, A. J., & Shackelford, T. K. (2015). Life seems pretty meaningful. *American Psychologist, 70*(6), 571.doi:10.1037/a0039209

Kumaran, S. (2018). World as Sanctuary: Philosophical perspectives on Amma Raj Joshi's Man and River. *International Journal of Multicultural Literature, 8*(2),16-25. ISSN:22316248

Merriam-Webster Dictionary (1828) on life-accessed on 09/20/2019

Metz, T. (2001). The concept of a meaningful life. *American Philosophical Quarterly, 38*(2), 137-153. Retrieved from http://www.jstor.org/stable/20010030-accessed on 09/18/2019

Morange, M. & Falk, R. (2012). The recent evolution of the question "What is Life" *History and Philosophy of the Life Sciences, 34*(3), 425-438. Retrieved from http://www.jstor.org-accessed on 09/15/2019

Purves, D., & Delon, N. (2018). Meaning in the life of human and other animals. *Philosophical Studies: An International Journal for Philosophy in the Analytic Tradition,175*(2), 317-338. doi:10.1007/s11098-017-0869-6

Repp, C. (2018). Life meaning and sign meaning. *Philosophical Papers,47*(3), 403-427. doi:10.1080/05568641.2018.1424027

Tiberius, V. (2013). *Recipe for a good life: Eudaimonism and the contribution of philosophy.* In A.S. Waterman (Ed.), The best within us: Positive psychology perspectives on eudaimonia (pp.19-38). Washington, DC, US: American Psychological Association. doi:10.1037/14092-002(/doi/10.1037/14092-002).

What is life? Question for the month. Philosophy Now (2019).

(Hopkins, pg 78)

Da Silva, D., & Murilo, C. (2016). *Suffering in Ecclesiastes: "This too id hevel"*. Concilium (00105236), 3, 55-66. Accession Number:116609930

Exline, J. J., Prince-Paul, M., Root, B. L., & Peereboom, K. S. (2013). The spiritual struggle of anger toward God: A study with family members of hospice patience. *Journal of Palliative Medicine, 16*(4), 369-375.doi:10.1089/jpm.2012.02.0246

Hasrat, D. (2019). Sources of meaning in life: A study of age and gender differences. *International Journal of Social Science Review, 7*(3),536-544. Accession Number:136139420

Henry, M. (May 1998,1991). *Commentary on the whole Bible.* (New Modern Edition). United States of America: Hendrickson Publishers, Inc.

https://biblehub.com/nlt/john/1-4.htm

https://livelifehappy.com/life-quotes/no-one-has-power-over-you/.

https://www.quora.com/What-is-the-estimate-of-king-solomons-wealth-in-todays-economy-and-is-he-the-likely-richest

Levicheva, L. I. (2014). *Contentment in the book of Ecclesiastes: Interplay of the themes of death, the role of God, and the contentment in Qoheleth's teaching.* Middlesex University (Dissertation). Accession Number: edsble.603351

Marcus, P. (2000). The wisdom of Ecclesiastes and its meaning for psychoanalysis. *Psychoanalysis & the Psychoanalytic Review, 87*(2), 227-250.

Metz, T. (2015). Fundamental conditions of human existence as the ground of life's meaning: Reply to Landau. *Religious Studies, 50*(1), 111-123. doi:10.1017/S0034412514000225

Newman, D. B., Schwarz, N., Graham, J., & Stone, A. A. (2018). Conservatives report greater meaning in life than liberals. *Social Psychological and Personality Science,10*(4), 494-503. doi:10.1177/1948550618768241. (Accession Number:2019-20707-008)

O'Donnell, D. S. (2014). *Ecclesiastes-Reformed Expository Commentary*. Phillipsburg, New Jersey: P&R Publishing

Pargament, K., & Hahn, J. (1986). God and the just world: Causal and coping attributions to God in health situations. *Journal for the Scientific Study of Religion, 25*(2), 193-207.

piezechukwu.blogspot.com/2018/04/the-5-unanswered-questions.html

Swami, J. (2015). Vanity Karma: Ecclesiastes, the Bhagavad-Gita, and the meaning of life-A cross-cultural commentary on the book of Ecclesiastes. *Journal of Ecumenical Studies*. Los Angeles, California: The Bhaktvedanta Book Trust International, p.338.

Tan, G. G. (2016). *The empirically corroborated theology of the meaning of life in Ecclesiastes: A biblical and empirical analysis with reference to Malaysian Businesspeople*. Prifysgol Bangor University (PhD Thesis). Retrieved from http//e.bangor.ac.uk.id/eprint/9822

The Bible
Wiersbe, W. W. (2001-2004). *The Bible Exposition Commentary: Old Testament*. Victor.

www.goodreads.com/author/quotes/17561

www.nancychristie.com/.../though-no-one-can-go-back-and-make-a-brand.

www.pinterest.com/pin/152770612346838665/